CISO Executive Primer

The Executive's Guide to Security Programs

Bill Bonney

Gary Hayslip

Matt Stamper

CISO DRG Publishing

Copyright © 2022 CISO DRG Publishing

CISO Desk Reference Guide Executive Primer
The Executive's Guide to Security Programs

ALL RIGHTS RESERVED

No part of this book may be reproduced, stored in a retrieval system, or transmitted in any form, or by any means whether by electronic, mechanical, photocopy, recording or otherwise, without the prior written permission of the copyright owner except in the case of a brief quotation embodied in a critical review and certain other noncommercial uses permitted by copyright law. For all other uses, requests for permission may be sent to the publisher, "Attention: Permissions Coordinator," at the address below:

>CISO DRG Publishing
>P.O. Box 928115
>San Diego, CA 92192-8115
><www.CISODRG.com>
>info@cisodrg.com
>ISBN 978-1-955976-05-3

DISCLAIMER: The contents of this book and any additional comments are for informational purposes only and are not intended to be a substitute for professional advice. Your reliance on any information provided by the publisher, its affiliates, content providers, members, employees or comment contributors is solely at your own risk. This publication is sold with the understanding that the publisher is not engaged in rendering professional services. If advice or other expert assistance is required, the services of a competent professional person should be sought.

To contact the authors, write the publisher at the address provided above, "Attention: Author Services."

Cover illustration and original artwork
by Gwendoline Perez

Copy editing by Nadine Bonney

Produced by Last Mile Publishing

Table of Contents

Foreword i
Preface v
   How to Use this Book viii
The Role of the Information Security Executive 1
   Introduction 3
   The CISO 5
      Executive Summary 6
      To Whom Should the CISO Report? 8
      The "Technical, IT-Focused CISO" Reporting to Traditional IT Leadership 9
      The Empowered CISO 10
      What Is the Future for the CISO Role? 16
      Key Insights and Recommended Next Steps 18
   Risk Management and Cyber Liability Insurance 21
      Executive Summary 22
      Defining Risk 24
      The Changing Risk Landscape 25
      Communicating Risk to Senior Leadership 26
      The Four Fundamental Ways to Manage Risk 28
      Where Does Cyber Liability Insurance Fit? 31
      Risks Covered by Cyber Insurance 34
      It's a Team Effort 35
      Key Insights and Recommended Next Steps 42
   Third-Party Risk 45
      Executive Summary 46
      Categorizing and Managing Third-Party Risk 48

What Is Our Third-Party Exposure? 49
Governance of Third Parties 51
Due Diligence 52
Contract Management 55
Provisioning and Implementation 56
Risk Monitoring 57
Performance Monitoring 57
Decommissioning 58
How to Assess and Work with Vendors Post Selection 58
Key Insights and Recommended Next Steps 60

Regulatory, Compliance and Audit 63
Executive Summary 64
Ensuring Good Compliance Outcomes 65
Legislation Is Changing Cybersecurity 65
Common Threads of a Cybersecurity Program 73
Build Compliance into Your Program 75
How to Engage with Your Auditors 77
Fixing the Relationship with Your Auditor 80
Key Insights and Recommended Next Steps 82

Data Governance and Security Policy 83
Executive Summary 84
What Data Is Important to Us and Where Is it? 85
Data Classification, Often Neglected 87
Not All Data Are Created Equal 89
Policy Is Foundational 90
Unintended Consequences 91
Policy Has a Purpose 93
Key Insights and Recommended Next Steps 94
Additional Information 95

Measurement and Reporting 99
Executive Summary 100
The Fundamentals of a Metrics Program 101
Metrics Principles 102
A Process Orientation 103

Business Objectives	104
Foundational Metrics	105
Administrative Metrics (Legal, Financial, HR)	106
Operational Metrics (Security and IT Operations)	108
Governance Metrics (Compliance)	109
Strategic Measurements	110
Key Insights and Recommended Next Steps	111

The Cybersecurity Program ... 113

Introduction ... 115

The Human Element ... 117

Executive Summary	118
Talent and the Human Element	119
Key Variables that Impact Recruiting Cyber Talent	120
Third-Party Service Delivery	121
Investing for the Long Term	122
Motivating Cybersecurity Professionals	123
Essential New Facets of Diversity	124
Awareness, Self-Defense, and a Shared Sense of Purpose	125
Historical Role Models	127
Use the Language of Business	128
Addressing Risk with Rigor	129
Does Training Really Work?	131
Key Insights and Recommended Next Steps	133

Situational Awareness ... 135

Executive Summary	136
Threat Intelligence	138
Continuity and Cyber-Resilience	144
Monitoring Your Environment	150
Key Insights and Recommended Next Steps	155

Incident Management ... 157

Executive Summary	158
Introduction	159
Phases of Incident Management	161
Preparation Is Key	161

Incident Management Requires Incident Governance 162
　　　The Purpose of Forensics 166
　　　Post-Mortem Review 166
　　　IT and OT Convergence: The Game Has Changed 168
　　　Key Insights and Recommended Next Steps 171

Executing the Cybersecurity Program 173
　　　Executive Summary 174
　　　Start with Knowledge About the Business 175
　　　Invest in People 178
　　　Be Strategic with Your Tools 180
　　　Budget and Strategic Plan 182
　　　Key Insights and Recommended Next Steps 184

Management and the Board 185
　　　Executive Summary 186
　　　The Board's Unique Role 188
　　　The Board Is Now a Target 189
　　　Guidance for Boards 190
　　　Evaluation of Incident Response Capabilities 190
　　　Review and Authorization of Budgets 192
　　　Adequacy of Insurance 192
　　　Ensuring Organizational Accountability 193
　　　Evaluation and Assessment of Controls and Disclosures ... 193
　　　The Unique Role of the CISO 194
　　　Tone at the Top 196
　　　Inform 197
　　　Collaborate 198
　　　Call to Action 199
　　　To Whom Am I Speaking? 199
　　　Key Insights and Recommended Next Steps 204

Bibliography 205
Data Categories and Examples 213
Acknowledgements 221
About the Authors 223

Foreword

The CISO Desk Reference Guide has been a mainstay in my personal library since shortly after I first met Gary, Bill, and Matt in 2015. Newly appointed to my second stint as Deputy Chief Information Security Officer (CISO) and having just moved from Germany to Southern California, I was eager to build relationships in the lively cybersecurity community of San Diego. The community welcomed me with open arms, and I was able to join in on robust conversations, insightful presentations, and war-room problem solving for the latest/greatest malware strain or threat actor activity. If I were to attempt an analogy, I would say reading the chapters of the *CISO Desk Reference Guide* is like attending a gathering of those fantastic SoCal professionals: approachable, unassuming, informative, and thought-provoking.

Since that wonderful season of my career based in San Diego, I've slingshot around the world to a variety of CISO and CSO positions, taking with me their *Reference Guide* (which I've also passed on to members of my leadership teams), their friendship, and their trusted comradery in this global cybersecurity war we as CISOs wage day in and day out.

Gary, Bill, and Matt are a treasure trove of wisdom for future and established CISOs alike. Their dedication to contributing foundational wisdom to the cybersecurity community has rightly earned their two-volume *Reference Guide* set a prestigious position in the Cybersecurity Canon Hall of Fame. What sets them apart is that they don't just "teach" the work, they also "do" the work. And by doing the work, they garner continuous insight and examples, which they then use to further teach the work. Theirs is a virtuous circle of support and insight for our cybersecurity community globally.

When the authors asked if I would be willing to read a draft and provide some feedback on the manuscript for their latest endeavor, *CISO Desk Reference Guide: Executive Primer*, I jumped at the opportunity. The premise of this *Executive Primer* is to assist non-cyber executives and non-execs in understanding the deep complexities of cybersecurity—without leaving their eyes watering from mind-numbing technical details. This is not a small task, but it is such important work. And this *Executive Primer*, as expected from the authors' previous work, does not disappoint.

As CISOs, we must leverage both "science" and "art" in the work we do every day. The science is the complexity, breadth, and depth of the processes, technology, and people capabilities that we must leverage, develop, and continuously improve every day to protect, detect, respond, and recover. The art is a bit more nuanced and requires tremendous skill and honing: every presentation to the Audit Committee and exec and non-exec boards, every meet/greet with business executives, every town hall presentation to non-cyber audiences, every "lunch and learn" session we host, every cyber threat briefing we send out to all hands—these are all examples of where we must demystify the "science" of our work, by using the "art" of communication, influence, connecting seemingly unrelated dots, all while using business-friendly lexicon and relevant, contextualized examples which broaden understanding while eliciting support, partnership, urgency, and priority.

In theory, a better understanding of cybersecurity by our non-cyber exec and non-exec colleagues will lead to greater support for the work of cybersecurity, healthier and courageous challenges in our conversations and dealings, and laser-focused risk prioritization by *you and me* as we together reduce risk. In practice, and for many, this is a foundational paradigm shift: everyone owns security. Not just the CISO or the CISO Program...everyone. You, dear Reader, own security.

But how can you own something and effectively participate in and contribute to your part of cybersecurity if you don't understand it, know why to prioritize it, or know what "good" looks like? Enter the *CISO: Executive Primer*. This Primer will get you well on your way to being familiar with and conversant in the work of the CISO Program at your company, just as we as practitioners and CISOs must be familiar with and conversant in your work, whether its finance, legal, HR, business imperatives, or company strategy. This *Executive Primer* will also give you a greater understanding of the story behind the story when you see a headline about the latest breach.

Personally, I believe you will come away with at least the beginnings of an understanding that cybersecurity is to no longer be a buried line item on IT's budget but to rather be seen as a prominent enterprise-wide, escalating risk that each exec and non-exec alike need to have in the forefront of her or his mind when they consider acquisitions, market expansion, product innovation, channels to market, interactions with shareholders, engagement with customers and consumers, leveraging third-party vendors, suppliers, and contractors, broaden their digital transformation, and so on.

I'm thrilled the authors have put pen to paper on this *Executive Primer*, and I highly recommend you chew through and digest all of this rich yet approachable content. To follow the analogy I began with, reading this *Executive Primer* is like having a lengthy coffee (or whiskey!) chat with Gary, Bill, and Matt, garnering their wisdom and insights in an approachable, unassuming, informative manner. I believe it will empower you for better, thought-provoking conversations with your CISO. I believe it will change the way you view risk at your company. And I believe you, too, will become a cybersecurity enthusiast at work and at home.

Kirsten Davies
May 2022
Nashville, USA

Kirsten Davies is a five-time Information and Cyber Security Executive, safeguarding 2 Global 100 and 3 Fortune 250 companies representing over $230Bn in annual turnover.

Preface

When Bill, Gary, and Matt met, the world had not yet begun to feel the daily pain that ransomware would become. In the halcyon days of 2014, celebrity breaches, meaning breaches we identify by name that often get their own nightly news coverage, were still new and rare. Nevertheless, cyber professionals could see what was coming. We'd been warning about lax security caused by underinvestment and poor oversight for years. For us, the U.S. off-price retailer TJ-Maxx (TJX) breach that began in 2005 was inevitable. In the TJX breach, hackers gained access through the company's wireless network by hacking the weaker wireless security protocol still in use at TJX at that time. After gaining access, the hackers retained access for approximately two years before being discovered. Only TJX and one other member of the 60 largest breaches of all time club, the Heartland payment processing company breach of 2008, occurred before 2012. By the time we published the first volume of the *CISO Desk Reference Guide* in July 2016, the club had reached 19 members. This book is not about breaches or malware strains or nation-state actors or eastern European crime gangs. Still, some of these breaches have proved to be catalysts for stepped-up attention and investment.

The Target breach in December 2013 showed how inattention to third-party service accounts, the infamous HVAC service connection, could provide a way in for criminals. Not even a year later, the Home Depot breach in September 2014 revealed that a company could be certified compliant for PCI-DSS (the payment card industry data security standard) and still have their payment systems breached. The Hollywood Presbyterian Hospital ransomware attack in February 2016 showed how holding operations hostage could cripple an enterprise. The SolarWinds breach in March 2020 demonstrated how critical and brittle the technology supply chain was and the Colonial Pipeline ransomware attack in May 2021 made clear how vulnerable our critical infrastructure really is.

In addition to the breathless media coverage, lawyers and regulators also began to take notice. In 2011, and then updated in 2018, the U.S. Securities and Exchange Commission began to require disclosure of potential material cybersecurity risks and cyber incidents in the Management's Discussion and Analysis (MD&A) and Risk Factors sections of the quarterly reports on Form 10-Q and annual reports on Form 10-K filed by public companies. Additionally, lawsuits following the Target breach named members of the board of directors as defendants. By May 2014, Gregg Steinhafel, who was Chairman, President, and CEO of Target at the time of the breach, had been removed from his posts. Though the early lawsuits targeting the board were not successful, taken together, these actions put the most senior leadership of organizations on notice.

Having fought the battle for relevance ourselves, we are keenly aware that Chief Information Security Officers (CISOs) spend a large portion of their time educating their colleagues in the C-suite about their mission, their role, the nature of the cyber threats we face, and what it takes to address them. We wrote this book to help provide context for the CISO's role so that senior leaders can understand how to help the CISO succeed in their mission and better grasp their own roles in making their organization more cyber resilient.

We use the term CISO throughout this book, and although this is an acronym for the specific job title of Chief Information Security Officer, you can think of it as shorthand for the highest-ranking information security executive in the organization. Other common titles include Chief Security Officer (CSO), Vice President of Information Security, Director of Information Security, and Director of Cybersecurity.

Similarly, we will often use the terms information security and cybersecurity somewhat interchangeably. There is a subtle difference. Information security is synonymous with data security and pertains to ensuring the confidentiality, integrity, and availability of data, in any form. Cybersecurity pertains to protecting data found on electronic devices and understanding what data is critical, where it is, its risk exposure, and how to protect it from cyber-attack.

How to Use this Book

The *CISO Desk Reference Guide Executive Primer* presents topics we first discussed in Volumes 1 and 2 of the *CISO Desk Reference Guide*. For readers of Volumes 1 and 2, you'll undoubtedly recognize much of this material. However, where Volumes 1 and 2 of the *CISO Desk Reference Guide* are designed to help CISOs and aspiring CISOs benefit from the experiences of seasoned executives who have walked in their shoes, the *Executive Primer* is written to include the CISO's colleagues and provide a C-suite perspective for both the security function and security executives.

This perspective is one of expectation. What are the expectations the CEO should have for their CISO? What resources should the CFO expect to provide the organization's CISO in support of their mission? What are the expectations the CISO will place on their colleagues to help make the organization more resilient? What kind of support should a CISO expect from the board? As important, what expectations should the entire leadership team, including the board, place on the CISO in terms of communications, teaching, expertise, risk assessment, metrics, meeting regulatory requirements, and preparing the organization to detect, respond to, and recover from cyber incidents?

Many of the examples in the *CISO Desk Reference Guide Executive Primer* have a U.S. orientation, though we do include international references when it is essential to illustrate the point. We assure you that global operations are not an afterthought. Still, given that this book relies more on principles than step-by-step instructions, we did not feel the need to extend lists and add examples merely to demonstrate inclusion.

We present the topics of the *CISO Desk Reference Guide Executive Primer* in two sections. There are six chapters in Section 1. After describing two models for the CISO position, we address the CISO's critical role in risk management, third-party risk, compliance and audit, and data governance. We conclude Section 1 by providing a window into the security metrics program for the organization. These topics can at times read like hygiene, but they represent essential investments of management's time and attention. Without a sound grounding in the risk, data governance, and regulatory and compliance disciplines, we lack the foundation necessary to build a strong security program.

In Section 2 we focus on the security program with an emphasis on a whole-of-enterprise approach. The five chapters in Section 2 address security talent and security awareness, developing situational awareness to provide the right context for data protection, preparing for and responding to the inevitable security incidents, security program execution, and the special role of the board and the board's unique relationship with the CISO.

Current CISOs would be well served to use the *Executive Primer* as a tool for developing closer partnerships with their C-suite colleagues and members of the board of directors, especially those who concentrate on the corporation's risk and resilience. Use particularly relevant chapters as conversation starters to explain your role or to start a dialog about a change that you're beginning to socialize or to put specific security programs into context.

Newly minted CISOs and security leaders who aspire to become CISOs will benefit from understanding senior leaders' expectations for CISOs. As we write in Chapter 1, "a higher profile almost always comes with greater expectations that the approach taken by the

CISO, on any given issue, will be appropriate from a C-level perspective, not just technically correct."

The CISO's colleagues in the C-suite and members of the board of directors can use the *Executive Primer* to gain critical insights about the challenges facing the CISO and the organization in a world where seemingly every corporate asset has a digital component and is increasingly under attack.

Throughout this book, we have tried to lay the groundwork for elevating the way we view cybersecurity programs. In 2011, Marc Andreessen famously said that software is eating the world. This is more than a provocative headline to us. The implication is that in the digital age, everything of value has a digital representation and therefore becomes a digital asset. How we protect digital assets is profoundly different than protecting physical objects. The information a piece of paper conveys, for example, may be exactly the same as a PDF file. Unlike the piece of paper, the PDF file can be many places at once. Every instance of the PDF file is uniquely available to use, to steal, or to destroy. Depending on the contents of the PDF file and rights the creator wishes to assert, it may be welcome or unwelcome in any one of the places it exists, it may be easier or more difficult to protect, and its existence may create new obligations on the custodian or custodians. As you read this book, we'd like you to keep in mind that this is the world of the CISO.

Section 1

The Role of the Information Security Executive

Introduction

In Chapter 1 we describe two different models for **empowering and managing the CISO**. Major topics include where and to whom the CISO reports, the level of responsibility entrusted to and expectations of the CISO, and insights about how we see the CISO's role evolving over time.

In Chapter 2 we begin a conversation about **risk**. We've referred to the CISO as the chief resilience officer, and helping lead the organization through risk assessment, risk management, and cyber insurance evaluation is a contribution we think CISOs are well-positioned to provide.

We continue the risk conversation in Chapter 3 by doing a deep dive into **third-party risk**. Well before the headlines about compromised technology supply chains, an enormous amount of risk had already been either wittingly or unwittingly transferred to third parties or arose because the relationships were often managed at arms-length with little oversight over how outsourced assignments were discharged.

As we wrap up the discussion on risk, Chapter 4 shifts the focus to **regulatory, compliance, and audit**. Fundamentally, these activities are concerned with the organization's governance of its external obligations and the management of its risks. The CISO's role includes both driving good compliance outcomes and performing an oversight function for the execution of IT General Controls (ITGC).

In Chapter 5 we look at the value and necessity of **data governance**. We begin by addressing the critical aspects of data classification and data mapping and outline the key types of sensitive and protected data. A significant proportion of information security policy directly relates to data governance, and we unpack that in the second half of Chapter 5.

We conclude Section 1 by addressing **measurement and reporting** in Chapter 6. In this discussion we bring the CISO's risk management duties full circle and show how the CISO works with his or her peers to ensure that operational decision making is fully risk informed.

In Section 2, we'll switch the focus to the execution of the cybersecurity program.

Chapter 1

The CISO

A great wind is blowing, and that gives you either imagination or a headache.

~ Catherine the Great

Executive Summary

Though relatively new for some organizations, the position of Chief Information Security Officer (CISO) is one of technical complexity and risk mitigation that is not for the faint of heart. This position is the leading cybersecurity expert for a company, and often faces repercussions if there is a data security breach. Incumbents will make decisions that impact all aspects of an organization and its ability to conduct business. Some of these decisions will involve interpreting regulations, establishing new policies, or influencing the employee/corporate culture. The reporting structure has a tremendous impact on the efficacy of the organization's security operations and the ability to influence culture. We believe that organizations with a designated security officer – a CISO – will have better security outcomes than those who have not yet formalized this role.

Where the CISO reports reflects how the organization views risk. Organizations that take an expansive view of cybersecurity and risk management will likely have a CISO reporting outside of traditional IT, perhaps to the CEO or CFO. This avoids having the CISO placed in the unenviable position of having to judge the work of their boss, frequently the CIO or CTO, and compete for a slice of the technology budget. Where the CISO reports also has critical implications for the security culture of the organization. This includes how security is viewed by employees and stakeholders and the ability of the CISO, the CISO's colleagues, and the security team to influence behavior and culture and drive change.

The CISO needs to know their organization's industry, regulatory requirements, and lines of business. This organizational context has significant implications for the security operations' staffing levels and budget. Organizations are demanding more of their CISOs. They expect CISOs to expand upon their in-depth technical knowledge of the organization's IT systems and applications to include domain expertise in risk management (including vendor risk management), and business operations and to be influential change agents.

We have labeled the CISO the CRO or Chief Resilience Officer. Over the last decade, we've seen the progression of thinking regarding the expectation that an organization will experience a cyber-attack shift from a mantra of "not if, but when" to an understanding that every digital asset is under continuous threat requiring constant diligence along with an acknowledgment that there will be failures and breaches from which the organization will need to recover. This new thinking makes organizational resilience a core competency in the digital age. These three disciplines, resilience, risk management, and change agent, are how we believe the CISO is best positioned to contribute to the organization beyond the foundational expectation of technical expertise. However, we must not underestimate the technical requirements and overburden the CISO such that technical diligence suffers.

Internal and external stakeholders, including CEOs, boards, and notably, standards bodies and regulators, require of the CISO an additional duty to speak plainly about the cybersecurity risks companies are facing and provide an accurate assessment of how these risks are being identified, tracked, and mitigated. The CISO's ability to discharge this duty fully is facilitated by allowing the CISO to maintain an appropriate separation of duties such that execution and validation of technical controls maintain separate reporting structures.

To Whom Should the CISO Report?

We often think of reporting relationships and organizational structures as fixed. Someone gets hired to do a job, reporting to a particular person in a department, business unit, or functional group with a specific structure, and learns to operate within those parameters. But as cybersecurity risks have become high-profile news-generating events, the role of the CISO has had to evolve. A higher profile almost always comes with greater expectations that the approach taken by the CISO, on any given issue, will be appropriate from a C-level perspective, not just technically correct. Along with the technical standards and regulatory requirements that CISOs are expected to master comes the requirement to know the products, the business, the customers, and the market in which the organization competes.

The CISO, regardless of reporting relationships, should provide guidance and expertise on the following:

- Cybersecurity practices, procedures, and metrics
- Data and asset classification from a cybersecurity and risk perspective (including privacy impacts)
- Vigilance and monitoring of cybersecurity activities and trends
- Oversight of auditing and governance practices including liaising with internal and external audit
- Incident response in collaboration with legal counsel
- Security policy design
- Security services implementation
- Security training
- Holistic risk management and risk assessment reporting (including vendor and business processes)

We describe two different models for the CISO role in the following passages.

The "Technical, IT-Focused CISO" Reporting to Traditional IT Leadership

When the CISO reports into a traditional IT structure, there is usually a more technical focus on cybersecurity activities. The CISO's primary function is to minimize the risks associated with IT services and to provide technical, cyber-related expertise to the CISO's colleagues within IT. Cybersecurity is network-centric, and core activities in this role center on device and network security. It's a dangerous world, and the CISO and his or her staff are there to ensure that only good data packets enter (or leave) the organization. Some refer to this approach as the "packet police." This is an overly simplified view of the CISO function to make the distinction more explicit when compared to the empowered CISO role discussed below.

There are substantial benefits from an IT-centric and technical approach to the CISO role. The cyber threats facing organizations today can be highly sophisticated attacks, and advanced persistent threats (APTs) require in-depth technical knowledge to discover and mitigate. Specifically, the CISO's team needs to understand packet analysis, network design and topology, and technical indicators of compromise (IOCs) to triage and respond to anomalous behavior within the organization. These skills and competencies are at the center of cybersecurity. An IT-centric CISO becomes a critical member of the IT leadership team, validating security configurations and practices.

Of concern with this reporting relationship, however, is the inherent conflict created by the reporting structure. If the CISO's core function is to ensure that IT security practices and configurations are managed correctly, communicating challenges with these practices upward in the organization (e.g., to the CISO's boss) can be problematic. The CISO is essentially asked to police his or her boss' work, evaluating the risk considerations created by the boss' selected technologies and their deployment. Such feedback can be career-limiting. For this structure to work correctly, the CISO and the CISO's boss must be open, professional, and focused on objective outcomes. Managing through the dynamic of questioning the IT leadership's practices, competencies, and policies puts an enormous strain on this role. This conflict is the reason why the separation of duties is such a necessary control.

Another challenge with this model is how the organization allocates budget money and budget authority to cybersecurity. Traditional metrics have related information security spend to a percentage of IT spend. While this can provide a useful rule of thumb and we list this as an example of foundational metrics in Chapter 6, this model can obscure essential factors that can have an inverse correlation to IT spend. These factors include, for example, the amount of technical debt the organization has accumulated, and the current and future cloud footprint. Both factors simultaneously generate savings in raw technology spend but require disproportionately larger investments in information security.

Where CISOs report organizationally is evolving to reflect these dynamics. Given the existential risks associated with poor cyber outcomes for many companies, the CISO function can no longer be buried two or three layers deep within traditional IT. Boards of directors and individual members of the C-suite have fiduciary requirements to manage their organization's risk. Not having accurate, complete, and timely detail related to cyber risk undermines this fiduciary responsibility. Consequently, we see a new CISO emerge. This modern CISO is a business partner and, ideally, a welcomed member of the C-suite.

The Empowered CISO

Key to this peer-based organizational structure is a broader, more holistic view of cybersecurity practices both within and outside the organization (think third parties and partners). Beyond the critical skills and competencies required to evaluate technical security matters, a CISO reporting outside of the traditional IT structure also needs additional context related to legal and regulatory issues.

The empowered CISO requires skills in combinations that are frankly hard to find and provide a limiting factor on this approach. This difficulty is one reason why there is intense competition for highly qualified CISOs in the market today. The empowered CISO must possess technical acumen across a variety of technologies and platforms, coupled with a deep, organization-wide understanding of risk management and privacy as well as legal and regulatory obligations.

Regardless of the model for the CISO role that works best for your organization, the following additional considerations apply.

Business Domain

For organizations under significant regulatory oversight, there is likely already robust organizational capability built up around complying with control requirements. Examples include the financial industry, pharmaceutical companies, defense contractors, and the healthcare industry. In many cases, corporate governance will be structured to comply with mandatory management oversight. This structure might consist of empowering specific committees of the board of directors with critical responsibilities and assigning particular members of the management team with formal roles in risk management and information security. Guidance from the Federal Financial Institutions Examination Council (FFIEC), the multi-agency bank regulator, requires an organization's board of directors to sign off on information security policy and business continuity planning. It also requires that information security officers report either to the board of directors or senior management to ensure appropriate separation of duties.

In these cases, the CISO must report at a level sufficient to provide appropriate oversight for key information technology strategy *and* execution. This would usually require that the CISO report to the CEO or a C-level executive. While reporting to the CIO, in this case, can work, this should be approached carefully as the guidance goes on to state: "Typically, the security officers should be risk managers and *not* a production resource assigned to the information technology department" (FFIEC, 2015) (emphasis added).

We believe the CISO should be endowed with sufficient independence to provide oversight for technical control execution. This starts with an appropriate reporting relationship. It also requires a careful bifurcation of technical control execution versus control testing and well-designed internal and external audit programs to provide an additional layer of checks and balances. Finally, to be able to speak plainly about cybersecurity risks and other technical risks to the business, the CISO must possess personal courage and develop the relationships and reputation that endow them with the gravitas necessary to be a trusted partner.

Also understand that attacking your organization may yield a disproportionate reward relative to other organizations. This could be because of name recognition, or perhaps your company provides a service that is critical to your customers' operations. Your organization may compete in an industry perceived as more susceptible to cyber-attack. These factors could put a larger target on your company, and you may have to structure your reporting relationship such that your CISO has a more prominent role. In these cases, besides crucial oversight of information technology implementation, the CISO may well be the critical escalation point to mobilize senior management, take control over multiple event responses, or even be the primary interaction point for communication channels. The CISO will need well-formed partnerships with key players on the incident response team. They might be juggling the immediate attack, news about that attack, and impacts on the organization's assets or customer/partner assets. Given the highly visible role, the CISO in this organization should probably report at the CEO or COO level.

To be successful, the empowered CISO needs to understand the organization's strategy, the information and data the organization handles, its lines of business and stakeholders, and the organization's overall risk appetite. The empowered CISO must also have solid interpersonal skills to work with colleagues across the organization who may view cybersecurity and associated controls as an impediment to acting. The CISO becomes the advocate in chief of good cybersecurity practices.

The empowered CISO needs to be seen frequently by non-IT members of the organization. An empowered CISO meets regularly with peers and department heads to understand their practices and their teams' needs from more than a cyber-specific perspective. As part of this management by walking around, the CISO learns about the organization's initiatives, stakeholders' objectives, shadow IT, non-IT sponsored applications, and key vendor relationships. This ground truth will provide important context for the CISO's cybersecurity activities. Equally important, having a highly visible CISO provides informal, but critical, opportunities for security training. These ad hoc discussions offer a knowledge transfer level rarely matched in more formalized security training efforts within an organization.

The empowered CISO will function in an advisory role within the firm. As such, the empowered CISO will weigh in on critical, potentially non-IT decisions, including vendor selection, data classification and treatment, mergers and acquisitions, and other activities that could impact the confidentiality, integrity, and availability of key systems supporting the organization. CISOs in this new role need to be highly effective communicators with notable powers of persuasion when formal authority is not entirely commensurate with the cybersecurity requirements at hand. These soft skills and influence usually require time to develop. CISOs must have the time and organizational commitment to grow into their roles.

Although most of this discussion has been about the CISO personally, the organization will not be able to accomplish its goals without structuring the rest of the information security department to complement the CISO's efforts. To allow the CISO to work with the GMs to develop that intimate understanding of business objectives, the senior leaders in information security must work with their peers to understand and influence the choices of key underlying technologies and development platforms. They should be keenly aware of significant milestones and deliverables. All the while, the security engineers must work with their counterparts in software development on threat models and secure coding methods for the development platforms that are in use. Members of the security operations team need to work with network engineers, database administrators, the helpdesk, and systems administrators to understand normal and anomalous usage patterns.

In addition to the in-depth subject matter expertise that security engineers must have, they must also be excellent team players. They should be capable of explaining security concepts in a way their development and support partners can consume. They should be well versed in the tools used by their peers, and most importantly, deeply aware of and supportive of their peers' deliverables. The business alignment of the CISO should cascade all the way down to the security operations team, and everyone in the security organization should focus on both their technical role and the business impact of their actions.

Skillset Alignment

We see the CISO role as having started later than other C-level roles but being on the same maturity path as the CIO. Like the CIO, the CISO is evolving from a purely or mostly role technical one to requiring strong business acumen. The CIO's role emerged from a business need to centralize technology management and add efficiency, reliability, and cost predictability to organizations' rapidly growing and ever more complex business technology footprint. The perceived risk addressed was that complexity, cost, and unreliability created a drag on the organization's competitiveness and profitability. Business leaders note that the successful CIO is first a business partner. As business partners, CIOs embrace and champion new delivery models such as cloud SaaS offerings and recognize the opportunity to take advantage of clustered expertise, capability, and innovation. They learn and improve from various forms of "shadow IT," incorporate into their portfolio what makes sense for their organization, and view all of the IT consumption models as part of their toolkit to enable the business to move with the speed and agility it requires.

Similarly, a C-level role for information security is evolving to allow organizations to bring order from chaos and provide leadership in a highly complex domain that cuts across all functional groups and business units. But many business leaders see the CISO emerging from a compliance-driven, risk-averse background and want to see evidence that the CISO can adequately balance risk versus reward and avoid establishing what they perceive as unnecessary barriers to success. Business leaders bear some responsibility for this perception.

Until recently, the CISO often went unnoticed until a breach occurred, and then was blamed and fired because of the breach. Still, the CISO must take several pages from the CIO playbook to truly learn the business and run their organization as a business. The CISO will need credibility with the business units to get the latitude to implement critical security controls and introduce the necessary rigor for successful continuity planning and cyber resilience.

What Is the Future for the CISO Role?

The future of cybersecurity will mature in parallel with the evolving tactics of cybercriminals and the accelerating change in information technology. Many of the new technologies such as cloud (in all its variants), software-defined networks (SDN), mobile technologies, Internet of Things (IoT), blockchain (or distributed ledgers), and quantum encryption will fundamentally impact the implementation of both networks and security programs. So too will the impact of "Remote First" or hybrid office/home workforce models build upon and accelerate the breakdown of the traditional secure network perimeter that began with the bring your own device (BYOD) model. These technologies and workforce interaction models will also be leveraged by cybercriminal organizations, resulting in new forms of digital crime not seen today.

The technologies mentioned above will substantially transform the role of the CISO. Some technologies which typically would be in the network operations portfolio will be consolidated under the umbrella of cybersecurity. Future CISOs will need to possess extensive knowledge of technology and how it applies to their business operations. The future CISO will need to assess risk continually as the organization integrates new technologies into disparate "legacy" corporate networks. These corporate networks will become more intertwined with the Internet – sharing, processing, and storing ever-expanding quantities of data. This data itself will evolve as more organizations adapt to the use of online social media platforms. Corporate "professional" data will merge with "personal" customer data, resulting in new data privacy requirements.

In this future view, network security, data privacy, physical security, and operations security will merge into a newly expanding business-focused cybersecurity portfolio. To effectively manage enterprise risk across this new portfolio of technologies, the future CISO will require a cybersecurity suite designed for continuous monitoring, alerting, and quick incident response. Security will become behavior-analytic driven as security teams employ tools that use data and threat analytics to proactively remediate security incidents. Should these potential security incidents develop into breaches, these tools will be instrumental in remediating the intrusion quickly and reducing the impact on business operations.

The organizations' perimeter will continue to change. The boundary will no longer be the physical or logical location of network assets but the location of corporate data, individual workers, and potentially, consumers. The CISO and their security program will become more focused on data – who has access (identity), what they are allowed to access (authorization), where to store it, and how to protect it. This data-centric view will become the new perimeter for the CISO to defend. Essentially, wherever the data is located is where security must be deployed. Taken to the logical extreme, everywhere in the ecosystem that data is created is a potential point of vulnerability and the CISO will want to consider what security controls can be deployed at each point. The new mantra for this view of security will be "total verification of identity and access," also known as "zero trust."

Cybersecurity is a service intertwined in all business operations, and it is incumbent upon the CISO to effectively manage this service and make it a valuable resource to their company.

Key Insights and Recommended Next Steps

The CISO should report to someone who can provide the right level of organizational support, visibility, and access to allow the CISO and cybersecurity program to successfully understand and mitigate risk by driving the necessary changes to corporate culture and behaviors. This arrangement should provide the CISO vital independence and provide:

- The ability to make recommendations and disagree with other technology leaders
- The ability to take a balanced, strategic view of deploying security controls
- Empowerment to fund, build and embed the cybersecurity program within the organization

To ensure the foundation within information security can support the time and attention the CISO must devote to educating and partnering with their peers, the CISO should work with the senior security leaders and empower them to partner with their peers throughout the organization. It is essential that they understand and influence the choices being made for key underlying technologies (including development platforms) and be keenly aware of significant milestones and deliverables.

Members of the senior leadership team, including members of the board where appropriate, should spend the necessary time with their CISO to make sure they are well informed about the organization's strategy, the information and data the organization handles, its lines of business and stakeholders, and the organization's overall risk appetite. The goal should be to equip the CISO to be a full business partner who would be welcomed into the C-suite.

The role of CISO is challenging. The CISO deals with an exceptional amount of risk tied to the company's business rules and technology portfolio. It will be the CISO's responsibility to assess the organization's risk exposure and provide alternatives that will protect the company, its assets, and its data. To do this effectively, CISOs will need to continually educate themselves about new threats and technologies, keep everyone informed, update the security program and policies, and use their entire stakeholder network. We believe that professional standards will continue to evolve and be codified to provide a true north that is distinct from technical standards and metrics. Further, we expect that corporations will need to extend protections currently afforded executive officers as accountability and consequences for security breaches continue to accelerate.

As Section 1 unfolds, it will become apparent that the foundational underpinning of any security program is provided by a clear-eyed approach to risk management and governance, made transparent by a metrics program that management comes to rely on as ground truth. What's clear is that the role of the CISO as the champion for cybersecurity and risk-mitigating activities has reached a level of importance that heretofore has not been seen within organizations. We are, in effect, entering the era of the CISO.

Chapter 2

Risk Management and Cyber Liability Insurance

All courses of action are risky, so prudence is not in avoiding danger (it's impossible), but calculating risk and acting decisively.
~ Niccolo Machiavelli

Executive Summary

The risk management function within organizations has changed considerably due to the dynamic threats facing enterprise business environments. Because there is more economic value embedded in computer networks and the systems they connect as we move more and more functionality online, there are more criminals attracted to cybercrime. At the same time, this march to online functionality exposes more systems to external threats. Not surprisingly, over the last few years, nation-states, industrial spies, and terrorists have begun to attack many more targets, endangering not just the largest enterprises but their supply chains as well.

Though not directly related to the subject at hand, the global pandemic that began in the last few months of 2019 and will likely extend through 2023 has combined with the increase in cyber-related disruptions to thrust both operational and supply chain resilience to the top of senior leadership's agenda.

Because of risk's enterprise-wide impact, we believe the modern CISO must have a deep understanding of their organization's industry, regulatory requirements, and strategic initiatives. This business context will provide critical insight for CISOs as they use their security program, policies, tools, and cyber insurance to better protect their organization and reduce its risk exposure to an acceptable level.

Another outcome of the expanding enterprise-wide risk profile is the impact that an adverse event can have on the organization. It is true that over the last few years large companies with significant financial resources have demonstrated the ability to withstand devastating cybersecurity breaches and continue as going and growing concerns. However, impacts far short of the organization's demise can be extremely detrimental. The fallout from adverse events such as cybersecurity breaches that involve personal data loss also includes lawsuits, settlements, regulatory investigation and sanction, loss of customers, and worst of all, the distraction of management while the organization recovers from the incident. The time and energy consumed are not then available for running the organization to the full benefit of its customers and shareholders.

As the impact from cyber events (especially ransomware[1]) continues to grow, evidenced by the year over year increases in the cost of a data breach,[2] so too does the cost and complexity of cyber liability insurance continue to rise. Understanding and configuring coverage and submitting claims as limitations and exclusions multiply creates a clear requirement for a multi-disciplinary approach to developing an organization's cyber risk management strategy.

Cyber liability insurance, which as recently as five years ago was a perfunctory purchase, is becoming fraught with its own set of risks. For mid-size companies, poorly managing coverage can expose the organization to spiraling premiums, high deductibles, and broadly applied exclusions that can make insurance contracts extremely onerous. For large multinationals, add to that the complexity of managing layers of coverage with a dozen or more providers that stitches together carriers by specialty and region. To address this issue, the CISO will need to work closely with finance and legal to ensure that cyber liability insurance remains part of the solution rather than another risk to manage.

---

[1] Ransomware attacks were $380,000 more expensive and were a factor in the breach 7.8% of the time - IBM's 2021 Cost of a Data Breach report.
[2] The highest increase in seven years (9.8%, from $3.86 to $4.24 million) – ibid.

Defining Risk

The National Institute of Standards and Technology (NIST 800-30 r1 2012) tells us that "risk is a function of the likelihood of a given *threat-source's* exercising a particular potential vulnerability and the *resulting impact* of that adverse event on the organization." Let's unpack these statements.

A *"threat source"* is an actor, in a cybersecurity context; these are hackers, hacktivists, industrial spies, malicious insiders, careless users, organized crime, terrorists, and nation-states.

Several factors need to line up to exercise a particular vulnerability. The organization must be exposed to that vulnerability, without adequate mitigation, and the threat actor must know (or be able to reasonably guess) that the vulnerability is there. How could a threat actor make a reasonable guess? Pack a malicious payload with multiple, frequently successful exploits and use multiple techniques to infest the target computers and then multiple techniques to gain control. As the criminal underground becomes aware of vulnerabilities, exploit kits such as Angler are updated to include these new attacks.

The *"resulting impact"* to the organization refers to a step beyond the immediate technical result, such as corrupting the compromised computer's hard drive (for instance, because of a ransomware attack), or establishing a link from the compromised computer to a command-and-control system outside the organization's control for later harvesting and data exfiltration. We're interested in the impact on the business. For example, the corrupted files mentioned above cause a productivity impact on the staff, or in some cases, impede some functions entirely until the files are decrypted, recovered from backup, or recreated. The infected computer, controlled by cybercriminals, can be used to collect personal information about customers or employees, commit fraud, expropriate intellectual property, or launch other more devastating attacks. These can be aimed at the organization itself, or the assets that are now controlled by cybercriminals can be added to a botnet rented out to the highest bidder to conduct malicious acts around the world.

The Changing Risk Landscape

Over the last few years, nation-states, industrial spies, and terrorists have begun to attack a greater range of targets. We have seen an increase in "steppingstone" attacks. Steppingstone attacks[3] involve stealing one piece of data from one victim to then steal something else from another. For example, cybercriminals carry out attacks to obtain social security numbers or PHI (protected health information) from one organization to file fraudulent tax refunds or fraudulent Medicare claims with another. A steppingstone attack makes more members of the value chain attractive targets. Because there is more economic value embedded in computer networks, there are more cybercriminals attracted to criminal cyber activity.

The rise of cybercrime syndicates and cybercrime eco-systems has also created a black market for specialized products and talents. Cybercriminals can procure lists of credit cards, collections of usernames and passwords, virus kits, exploit kits, and zero-day vulnerabilities from various sources. All of these can come complete with customer service, consulting, contract labor for customization, call centers, and boiler pits to "work" the leads (victims).

A third and equally crucial changing factor in the risk function is the impact of the adverse event on the organization. The example of ransomware noted above is quite disruptive to the organization while it is recovering the infected files and dealing with likely reputational

---

[3] Our term of art, introduced in the *CISO Desk Reference Guide, Volume 1*, Chapter 7 – Risk Management and Cyber Liability Insurance, CISO DRG Publishing, Bonney, Hayslip & Stamper.

damage and the exfiltration of its data. But the fallout, as we mentioned, can be devastating to management focus.

In the past, cybercrime affected mostly large companies who often had relatively poorly secured systems. The combination of unsophisticated attack tools, relatively few bad actors (compared to current numbers), and the natural lag for smaller firms in interconnecting operations skewed the risk function toward larger companies and comparatively more modest losses. In the recent past, "it won't happen to us" or "we can handle that level of loss" were common sentiments. "It won't happen to us" is a statement of the likelihood that a threat source would exploit a potential vulnerability. "We can handle that level of loss" designates the resulting impact as acceptable and not worthy of additional mitigation.

Communicating Risk to Senior Leadership

In trying to educate executives and boards, information security professionals have focused too much on the technical aspects of the "it won't happen to us" side of the equation. We discuss system vulnerabilities and programmatic attacks without adequately setting the context of the business reasons why the likelihood is going up (i.e., the changing risk/reward equation for cybercriminals) and the rising business impact (for example, disruptions in the technology supply chain) of successful attacks. Without this context, it has been difficult to inspire the changes in behavior required to address the growing risks.

In trying to address this, some information security professionals have focused on the ROI of security programs versus the impact of cyber incidents. It is undoubtedly a good idea to focus on ROI, but the calculations are often subject to error. One contributing factor is misunderstanding the changing values for the likelihood of incidents as the number of actors, the number of vulnerabilities, and the economic incentives of cybercrime continue to increase. Another is drastically underestimating the cost in time, focus, and money of recovering from an actual breach.

Most information security professionals have accepted as axiomatic the near certainty of a breach for well over a decade, but the executive team has only recently been starting to agree. Worse, very few organizations can successfully determine the organization's likely cost if a breach were to occur. Insurance companies continue to charge a wide range of premiums for policies. With each new breach, another collection of publicity-minded and litigation-prone groups comes forward with a point to make. As we've seen, compensating individuals for exposing their data, paying the regulator's fines, and replacing credit cards, though costly, are no longer the most significant cost factors.

Also, many biases impact our reasoning when we are less than sure of the outcomes. These biases, such as the status quo bias (taking the current state as a baseline), present bias (valuing current certainties over future uncertain outcomes), and the overconfidence effect (rating ourselves better than objectivity would suggest is warranted) operate against us when we are not confident of our facts or the outcome of our actions. When we attempt to explain the risks and the changes in behavior we're advocating for in response to these threats in a non-technical way, it often leads to over-simplification, which is reinforced by the media's constant over-dramatization.

These factors conspire to make it extremely difficult to motivate an executive team to change behavior if we cannot frame the reasons for doing so in business terms. One of the critical responsibilities of the CISO is to educate the executive team on the business impact of cybercrime. Explaining first what a cyber failure will do to the bottom line puts the discussion about countermeasures in the proper context. "To avoid disruption to the supply chain during the holiday season, we're taking the following steps…" is a more motivating action plan than "To avoid malware attacks, we're forbidding employees to use their work laptop for holiday shopping." Trust among executives is key, especially when it comes to a shared understanding of business imperatives. We know there has been a decades-long journey the CIO has been on to gain his or her peers' trust. There is perhaps a greater sense of urgency for the CISO to make that journey more quickly because the perceived risk of attack is more visceral than the risk of costs spiraling out of control or missed opportunities in data management and exploitation.

The Four Fundamental Ways to Manage Risk

Figure 2.1 Four Methods of Risk Management

There are four fundamental ways of managing risk: avoid the risk by exiting the business, mitigate the risk with various methods to counter the threat, transfer the risk by contracting for insurance or with partners to share the consequence, and accept the risk as a natural outcome of doing business.

Let's start to unpack these risk management approaches. The first, and the one most often associated with the CISO, is avoiding the risk by not allowing the business activity to take place. It's become almost cliché by now to refer to the CISO as "Dr. No" or "The Corporate Cop." However, it's incumbent on the CISO to help the organization "get to yes" and speak to the executive team in "the language of business."

There certainly are situations when the best thing for the organization is to avoid a particular risk. It is also true that sometimes this is because of technical, security-related issues that the CISO may have been best positioned to recognize. But to work with senior leaders effectively and guide the decision to avoid a particular risk, the CISO must first build the necessary trust by partnering with the business. The CISO should work with the business to execute smart, secure strategies within business processes that involve new technologies when the business begins to experiment with them. In this way, mitigation strategies might replace unfortunate avoid decisions (or misguided avoidance strategies) that unnecessarily hinder the business.

Let's move on to mitigation as the second fundamental way of managing risk. There are more ways to mitigate risk than just using technical controls, even in the domain of information security. Certainly, patching, keeping up to date on releases, and continuous testing and monitoring, including penetration testing, are critical technical mitigation activities. However, as many of us have learned the hard way, not every system is a good candidate for patching and upgrades.

Some technology platforms have exceeded their useful life, making systems and applications running on those platforms unusually brittle or rendering patches and upgrades unavailable. This is often referred to as technical debt (aka tech debt). To be successful here, the CISO should understand the particular business impacts that adverse events exploiting these vulnerabilities can cause, the cost of those impacts (such as hard costs, opportunity costs, and brand impact), and the cost to implement additional mitigation. This understanding will help prioritize the more challenging systems and at the same time help make the case to a skeptical executive that the impact of downtime on operations is a worthwhile investment to mitigate the potential exploitation of a vulnerability. Another potential outcome is elevating the upgrade priority for the underlying systems or paying down a portion of the technical debt.

Other technical mitigation strategies are often available. Understanding the complete environment in which a system operates, along with good working partnerships with the CIO staff and business teams, can lead to designing solutions that no single group could devise on its own. The outcome: reducing the probability of exploitation from a vulnerability to an acceptable level given the likely impact if successfully exploited is more important than the particular method or group responsible.

Not all assets are created equal. The CISO should prioritize with stakeholders which assets require the most protection and the focus of the cybersecurity risk management program. To do this, the CISO could use asset classification to decide the level of protection dedicated to an asset based on its class and value. Organizations tend to overprotect assets and data that have limited inherent value while under protecting assets that are effectively the 'crown jewels' for the organization. It's counter-intuitive, but this is often what causes failures – safeguards collapse under the burden of protecting everything. It is crucial to understand which assets make up the category of "most valuable assets" as prioritized by the business stakeholders. This means that all stakeholders must assist in prioritizing what is important to them. A good rule of thumb to help the organization in this process is to ask, "if these assets are stolen, compromised, misused, or destroyed, would this result in significant hardship to the organization?" If the answer is yes, then they are critical assets and will require added protection.

Where Does Cyber Liability Insurance Fit?

We turn now to the final two risk management options: for risks we cannot avoid or mitigate we must either transfer or accept the risk. Typically, transfer of risk involves a contract of some sort. To transfer the risk of currency fluctuation, for example, you could purchase a currency hedge. To transfer the risk of running afoul of employment law, you could outsource the performance of human resource functions to a firm specializing in these functions, with explicit guarantees of outcomes compliant with applicable laws and regulations.

The final option for managing risk is to accept the risks we cannot avoid, mitigate, or transfer. There are plenty of valid reasons to "self-insure," and prudent risk management should address this question with a data-driven approach. As we mentioned above, many biases impact our reasoning when we are less than sure of outcomes. Using a data-driven approach can help your organization avoid falling victim to these biases.

There should be an impact analysis conducted for each risk that the organization decides to accept. Even if it's a relatively high-level analysis, be aware of the impact to the organization if an adverse event occurs. Low probability, low impact risks might be easy decisions and are generally good candidates for risk acceptance, except where compliance and effective risk mitigation is legally mandated. Risks that come with potentially high impacts require more thought and discussion. While reviewing the potential impact of an adverse event, assess whether the organization is prepared to respond if the event occurs. Contingency plans and recovery plans should be in place as appropriate, including having contracts in place for backup facilities, backup data centers, and alternative vendors whenever possible.

Transfer of risk is also the foundation of insurance transactions. When you enter into an insurance contract, you take a specific risk, or basket of risks, all spelled out precisely in the insurance contract, and transfer that risk from the policyholder to the insurer in exchange for a premium. It's important to recognize that the only portion of the risk being transferred via insurance is the cost. You cannot transfer the risk of an adverse event occurring, but you can transfer certain portions of the monetary impact to the insurance company.

When insurance is thought of in the context of enterprise risk management (ERM), how we look at cyber insurance can be evaluated and weighed against other alternative risk-management actions.

CISOs can help provide critical context for the C-suite and board around the organization's cyber exposure. Specifically, understanding the total maximum exposure should a breach occur. While there are many approaches to addressing this, there are some necessary benchmarks that can quantify the organization's risk. The simplest method is to look at the organization's data and determine the approximate count of the number of records that have PHI, PII, or cardholder data. These are all data sets that have required actions should a breach occur. Numerous studies from the Ponemon Institute and empirical data from cyber insurance carriers who have had to pay claims suggest that the cost per record compromised ranges wildly. Still, an average of between $150 and $200 per record should suffice as an estimate.[4] Suppose an organization has 100,000

---

[4] What's new in the 2021 Cost of a Data Breach Report (https://securityintelligence.com/posts/whats-new-2021-cost-of-a-data-breach-report/)

records with data that would require an appropriate response (e.g., notification letters or credit monitoring), and the estimated cost per record compromised is $150. In that case, the organization has a potential loss of $15 million. This amount is just the possible loss resulting from one incident should all records be compromised. Many organizations have had multiple, significant incidents within a single calendar year.

Beyond the fundamental cost-per-record metric, the C-suite and board will also want to understand other contractual obligations and the associated exposure. To help address this context, working with the organization's legal counsel is invaluable. Tie this contractual review to specific client and vendor relationships or contracts required by regulation such as the business associate agreement (BAA) used between covered entities and their vendors (business associates) that have access to PHI, as is the case in the healthcare sector. Evaluate covenants within these contracts regarding the overall financial exposure should a cyber event occur. There may be other breach notification clauses related to the stewardship of PII in the organization's possession. Historically, contracts between organizations did not commonly require specific minimal security practices and controls to be in place (e.g., adopting the NIST Cybersecurity Framework, ISO 27001, or the Center for Internet Security's Critical Security Controls), but this is changing.

There will also be questions relating to current cybersecurity practices and their effectiveness in mitigating or reducing risk. CISOs will need to provide up-to-date status on how well the overall cybersecurity program is functioning. Complement this update with data-flow diagrams (DFDs) showing how sensitive information moves into and out of the organization and which applications and individuals can access this data. These DFDs, coupled with an accurate record count, will help the C-suite and the board estimate the organization's overall financial exposure.

Risks Covered by Cyber Insurance

Cyber insurance covers two distinct categories of expenses: first-party expenses (the organization's specific expenses) and third-party claims (the exposure to claims against the organization given a breach or other such incident). The CISO should work with the legal and finance teams to develop a strategy of exactly which risks to lay off through insurance contract. The more mature the company and its overall financial risk mitigation expertise, the more it will wish to consider a hybrid approach and designate specific potential harms for coverage. As this strategy is developed, risk reduction opportunities should be identified and prioritized as appropriate.

First-party expense coverage is designed to cover those expenses that are tied directly to the organization, including cyber extortion coverage, business interruption coverage, and other business-related expenses associated with the breach. The latter includes items such as the costs of digital forensics and the hard costs associated with breach response (customer notifications, credit monitoring services, increased staffing to field client inquiries – crisis management, if you will).

Third-party expense coverage addresses penalties and regulatory actions related to privacy and security violations resulting from the inadequacy of privacy and security protections within the organization. Third-party coverage may also include content-related issues, including copyright infringements, libel, and slander. Policies generally have coverage limits, with sub-limits for specific first-party and third-party damage. We highly recommended that a qualified insurance broker assists with validating what each insurance provider's policy covers and to what extent. The cyber insurance marketplace is becoming more mature, yet losses tend to increase asymmetrically as high-profile breaches (including ransomware attacks) are not evenly spread across providers. Therefore, vetting several carriers should be the norm – try to get quotes from at least three underwriters.

As part of the policy due diligence, it's essential to validate explicit exclusions and effective date clauses. Given how nuanced this type of insurance may be, a given exclusion could be the difference between a policy that has value to the organization and one that should never have been purchased. Similarly, we know that it can take months to discover a breach. Sophisticated attacks are extremely difficult to detect and often go unnoticed for half a year or more.[5] Work closely with the broker to ensure that there is some retroactive date available with the policy.

A good practice is to create a simple matrix that outlines the critical variables associated with each policy, including aggregate limits, sublimits, exclusions, and effective (retroactive) dates along with associated costs. Cyber liability insurance varies in the cost of coverage more notably from carrier to carrier than other types of insurance, so really work with your selected broker to vet the options carefully. Caveat emptor has never been more critical than for this type of purchase.

It's a Team Effort

Cyber liability applications require input from the CISO and CIO to address current security and IT practices and from the Chief Privacy Officer to help validate the extent of the organization's PII, cardholder data, or ePHI record counts. There are also sections within most applications for human resources, including questions related to hiring practices, background checks, and training. Some particularly challenging questions relate to known past cyber events.

---

[5] In 2021 it took an average of 212 days to identify a breach - IBM's 2021 Cost of a Data Breach report.

Applications typically require the signature of an executive officer of the organization. There is also a section that discusses insurance fraud in the case that information is knowingly withheld from the application. The application requires collaboration between multiple organizational domains – including human resources, security, IT, vendor management, and privacy departments. It is a red flag if the organization does not involve the CISO with the application process.

Some key cyber liability insurance provisions and terms are as follows:

Trigger – Loss/Claim: Cyber policies are triggered by either a loss of data or a claim. The claim comes from an event experienced by the organization and reported to the insurance company.

Claim type policies are more restrictive concerning events that could trigger the coverage of the policy.

Loss type policies are preferable; however, the cost of coverage will be higher.

Trigger – Defense: A cyber policy where there is a "defense" obligation triggered by a suit or claim. This requires a lawsuit or written demand against the insured (the organization). The policy may preclude reimbursement for the defense of a claim that has not evolved into a lawsuit or written demand. You would want less restrictive defense language and in some cyber policies the "suit limitation" doesn't apply to government action or investigations.

Defense – Choice of Counsel: Some cyber policies only cover defense costs to a certain extent, and the insured is required to choose from a list of the insurer's "panel" of law firms. The insured would ideally have input in the choice of counsel. You should look for policies with balanced "choice of counsel" language, such as aiming for the insured and insurer to agree on counsel, and if they cannot, the insured selects who they wish, and the insurer pays up to a specific amount.

Retroactive Coverage: Losses arising from events before the retroactive date are not covered. Insurers often fix the retroactive date at the initial date of coverage. You may be able to negotiate a date further back in time, but this will be at significant cost due to the risk to the insurer.

Acts and Omissions of Third Parties: Acts/omissions of third parties may be partially covered or excluded. Some cyber policies provide coverage for breaches of data between the insured and third parties (typically you will have a written services agreement between the insured and the vendor). If the organization has sensitive data retained by a third-party vendor (e.g., cloud storage) you should seek a policy that expressly covers breaches of data maintained by third parties.

Coverage of Unencrypted Devices: Many policies exclude coverage for data lost from unencrypted devices. Coverage without this requirement is preferable.

Coverage for Corporations and Other Entities: Cyber policies define "covered persons" for liability purposes as a "natural person." However, entities affected by data breaches can be corporate and business entities. Ensure coverage properly defines the scope of entities affected by a data breach.

Policy Territory – Occurrence Outside Country: The insured may not have operations outside of their home country. What happens if an employee loses their laptop or device while traveling abroad? Policies may restrict applicable coverage territory to the home country and its territories. Verify that your coverage is not this restrictive. Some cyber policies may only cover data loss if it was electronic data, versus paper printouts or reports. You should ensure coverage is for a data breach that involves both electronic and non-electronic records.

Location of Security Failure: Coverage for some policies is only for theft of data from company premises. This could be an issue if you have theft of data from a laptop at an airport. Some policies also limit coverage of data breaches from password theft to situations where credentials have been obtained through only non-electronic means. This doesn't consider the theft of credentials online and leveraging them for access. The organization should assess these limitations; be wary of them because they don't consider the new threats companies are facing today.

Exclusions for Generalized Acts or Omissions: Some policies may exclude coverage for losses arising from shortcomings of the security program which the insured was aware of before purchasing the policy, or the insured's failure to take reasonable care. Exclusions for this issue can be overly broad and lack adequate definition. They can potentially be subject to how the insurer wants to apply them. We suggest they be limited appropriately through negotiation or removed entirely.

Exclusions for Acts of Terrorism or War: This is a common type of exclusion added to a policy. It can be unclear the extent to which the insurer will want to leverage this exclusion if a cyber incident is due to the activities of a foreign nation or hostile foreign organization. The breadth of this exclusion should be negotiated. If that's not feasible, we recommend that the organization consider alternative secondary insurance coverage. As nation-states continue to use directed attacks and cause collateral damage that affects private entities to create leverage on the host government, insurance coverages and exclusions will continue to evolve. Jon Bateman wrote an excellent piece for the Carnegie Endowment for International Peace[6] that lays out the dilemma quite well. We suggest that the

---

[6] War, Terrorism, and Catastrophe in Cyber Insurance: Understanding and Reforming Exclusions (https://carnegieendowment.org/2020/10/05/war-terrorism-and-catastrophe-in-cyber-insurance-understanding-and-reforming-exclusions-pub-82819)

organization's risk management function monitor developments in this area and adjust their risk register appropriately.

Liability insurance is purchased by the organization (first party) from the insurer (second party) for protection against the claims of another (third party). Organizations can purchase cyber insurance for themselves, internally, and for protection against claims from third parties.

The coverage and features commonly offered for *first party (internal) cyber insurance* are as follows:

Theft and Fraud – covers certain costs for the theft and/or destruction of the organization's data and the theft of the organization's funds.

Forensic Investigation – covers the cost of determining the cause of the loss of data. Note that in some cases, the insurance carrier requires the insured to use only approved forensic team and breach response teams. This needs to be incorporates into your IRP.

Network Business Operation – covers the costs due to the interruption of the company's computer systems. Some policies require an "intentional cyber-attack." Be aware that internal staff can cause interruptions due to maintenance mistakes, or by using legacy equipment. Some policies may have limitations on interruption coverage, including minimum interruption before triggering, or total length of coverage calculated after the trigger goes into effect. The total length of coverage requires special attention because the length of event can vary widely based on the cause. For example, events caused by simple misconfigurations are far easier to detect and are resolved much faster than events caused by compromised credentials.

Extortion – covers the cost of "ransom" if third-party entities demand payment to refrain from releasing information to the public or causing damage to the organization's critical digital assets.

Data Loss Prevention – covers the cost of restoring data that is lost and diagnosing or repairing the cause that precipitated the loss. This will have some limits on the size of data to recover and the cause of data loss that the policy will pay to repair.

The coverage and features commonly offered for *third-party cyber insurance* are as follows:

Privacy Liability Coverage – liability to insured customers, clients, and employees if there is a breach and loss or damage of private information. The organization should seek to have the trigger language of the insurance policy focus on the insured's failure to protect confidential information, regardless of cause, versus language which states, "intentional breach." The insurance policy should provide coverage for insured's failure to disclose a breach under applicable breach notification laws, provide defense from the earliest stages of an investigation, and include requirements for civil investigative demand (requests from regulators and governments).

Regulatory Action – there is substantial variation among cyber insurance policies regarding coverage for regulatory or government action. Some policies require initiation of a formal complaint before a "trigger of coverage." This can be problematic because it would preclude reimbursement for the defense of the investigative stage (forensic investigation) of a regulatory or government action. This is typically the most expensive stage for an organization under investigation. Policies that include defense from the earliest stages of the investigation are preferable. Civil fines and penalties are covered under most cyber insurance policies.

Notification Costs – these are the costs of notifying third parties who may be affected by a data breach. Most cyber insurance policies provide this coverage. Many policies limit the number of persons who may be notified and the methods of notification. Some policies may vest some control over the notification process with the insurer.

Crisis Management – coverage should include the cost of managing the public relations fall out of a data breach. Most policies have some form of coverage for this. Many require the insured to choose from a list of vendors provided by the insurer.

Call Centers – this portion of a cyber insurance policy may be covered within the notification or crisis management coverages. This coverage can be purchased separately. Be advised that this tends to be one of the highest costs in a data breach investigation. Limitation on the number of affected people who are eligible to receive the call center services, hours and locations of the call center, and the specific services the call center will provide are common.

Credit or Identity Monitoring – included in most cyber insurance policies, it typically states that it is limited as to the number of affected people who can receive services and the insured may be required to pick from a prescribed list of vendors.

Transmission of Viruses or Malicious Code – coverage protects against liability claims alleging damages from transmission of viruses and other malicious code/data. Not all policies will have this coverage, so before requesting it, you need to consider how likely it is that your systems could be a source of this type of liability.

Cyber liability insurance remains a relatively new form of insurance compared to other forms of business coverage, notably general liability. With the explosion of ransomware incidents and more data (incidents) to inform actuary tables, the costs of cyber incidents have resulted in a notable increase in policy premiums. In some cases, nearly doubling.[7]

---

[7] Cyber insurance premiums, costs skyrocket as attacks surge, TechTarget Oct 2021 (https://www.techtarget.com/searchsecurity/news/252507932/Cyber-insurance-premiums-costs-skyrocket-as-attacks-surge)

Key Insights and Recommended Next Steps

CISOs are quickly becoming a critical part of the organization's risk management team and depending upon the industry in question, the CISO may function as the organization's Chief Risk Officer. CISOs should embrace this role. It broadens their perspective on their organization and their industry and facilitates greater cooperation and collaboration with their peers. They should be comfortable with and embrace good risk management. However, avoid the trap of allowing the organization to put the burden of risk acceptance entirely on the CISO. Their job is to help the leadership team understand the risks and make thoughtful decisions about the risks to which the organization is exposed.

CISOs need to express cyber risk in business-accessible terms. Describing threats and vulnerabilities in technical jargon will almost assuredly result in confusing the audience. Make sure that everyone understands the organization's current risk environment even if there is disagreement on approaches to minimizing the identified risk.

Risk management requires the CISO to work and collaborate with individuals across the organization and not just with their colleagues in IT. There must be an information exchange between all members of the senior leadership team. Knowing the business impacts of the organization's cyber risks will help translate cyber risk into enterprise risk terms. This, in turn, will help ensure that the entire leadership team understands the cyber risk mitigation requirements. CISOs and their peers should spend the time needed to develop a full understanding about which systems, processes, and activities are essential to qualify and quantify the risk exposure.

Cyber insurance has become an important tool in the organization's risk management toolbox. Cyber insurance policies may cover both first-party and third-party expenses and should be evaluated and assessed on their respective coverage limits and sub-limits. Given the complexities of cyber liability coverage, we recommend that you use an insurance broker to help determine which type of policy is appropriate based on the organization's workloads, risk appetite, and budget.

As the organization's risk management matures, new considerations can be added into the decision-making process with respect to the exact configuration of the organization's cyber liability policies. The prevalence of ransomware attacks combined with the increasing involvement of nation-states and nation-state affiliated actors in cyber-attacks that impact commercial interests are driving up policy premiums and deductibles and causing exclusions to proliferate. A hybrid approach that combines specific risks to offload with programs designed to limit the frequency and impact of other risks can generate cost reductions and help shift management's focus from managing contracts to driving improvements. Cyber liability insurance should always be thought of as a part of the overall risk mitigation strategy.

Senior leadership and the board should be laser focused on cyber resilience to blunt the increasing impact of adverse events on the organization. We'll cite the example of ransomware again. As we noted, the fallout from cybersecurity breaches that involve personal data loss includes lawsuits, settlements, regulatory investigation and sanction, loss of customers, and the distraction of management. The board would be well-served to take direct interest in the organization's ability to detect and recover quickly from cyber incidents.

Chapter 3

Third-Party Risk

Upon the conduct of each depends the fate of all.
~ Alexander the Great

Executive Summary

The reality is that most organizations do not have a good understanding of the cybersecurity risks they are assuming with their third-party relationships. This reality was exposed by the now-infamous Target and Snowden breaches, both in 2013. In the Target breach, access was obtained by the bad actors through the VPN connection maintained for Target's HVAC vendor for direct billing purposes. For the Snowden incident, Edward Snowden was an employee of a subcontractor of the National Security Administration. He moved from the CIA to Dell to Booz Allen Hamilton under a veil of suspicion after trying to break into classified files while at the CIA, and later fled with a trove of classified information. If we needed further convincing, in March of 2020, the SolarWinds software build process was compromised, providing a backdoor into more than 18,000 customers of its Orion Network Management System.

As a consequence of these breaches, organizations, regulators, and auditors now pay additional attention to third-party relationships, and the CISO will inherit a lot of the responsibility that comes with that additional attention. Even before these breaches, some industries have historically had key controls to address third-party risk. These include, for example, the banking industry, where firms must identify, assess, and track critical third parties, and healthcare, where business associate agreements (BAAs) must be in place and cascade (but do not transfer – the covered entity remains accountable) responsibilities to each party that handles protected health information (PHI).

Third-party relationships include, at a minimum: contractors, consultants, vendors, partners, and suppliers. Though similar in some ways, these represent five distinct types of external relationships with potentially very different kinds of risks. Contractors, consultants, and vendors offer mainly back-office contributions.

Partners and suppliers often provide go-to-market, production, or manufacturing contributions. In this sense, contractors, consultants, and vendors are bottom-line contributors, and partners and suppliers are top-line contributors. The distinctions between different types of third parties is highlighted further with the California Consumer Privacy Act (CCPA) and the California Privacy Rights Act (CPRA). In this case the distinction is made between service providers and all other third parties for the purpose of so-called "Do Not Sell" provisions allowing consumers to opt-out of having the information sold (and coming soon, shared) by the original data collector.

It's essential to understand how the business depends on its third parties to provide the right context for the risk assessments and subsequent risk management decisions that must be made regarding those relationships. Critical aspects of the risk assessments include the classification and lifecycle of data that flows between the organization and its third parties, the confidence management can place in the third party's security controls, and their resilience in the face of disruptions to their operations.

While we focus most of our attention in this chapter on the routine governance of third-party relationships, it is critical that we do not let the heat of battle cause us to fail in our responsibilities to safeguard private information. Mishandling of private information while responding to a crisis, perhaps by using a third-party provider that we have failed to properly vet or by simply assuming an existing partner has quickly implemented the necessary controls to handle a new type of private data, can subject us to the same negligent outcome as a failure of our own poorly controlled process.

Categorizing and Managing Third-Party Risk

In Chapter 2, we addressed risk management as a critical component of the cybersecurity function. In this chapter we will look at the CISO's role in an organization's management of a specific kind of risk, that of third-party risk.

Many of the risks involved with employing third parties center around the "unknown" – the lack of visibility into their operations, network environments, and corporate culture. There are five high-level categories that we can use to discuss the level of risk that is present with third parties.

1. *Financial Risk* – risk of the third party's continued financial viability

2. *Strategic Risk* – risk imposed on the organization from the third party's poor business decisions or failure to respond appropriately to a new competitors' arrival or other changing market conditions

3. *Operational Risk* – risk imposed on the organization because the third party is experiencing challenges in conducting normal business operations

4. *Regulatory/Compliance Risk* – risk that arises due to a third party violating laws, rules, or regulations, or due to lack of compliance with the organization's internal policies or procedures

5. *Geographic Risk* – risk imposed on the organization when it uses third parties who provide products and services from geographic regions outside of its own country or region

We should include three additional risk categories inherent to technology:

1. *Privacy Risk* – risk imposed because of the type of data shared with the third party, including PII and PHI. This often comes with additional legal and regulatory/compliance risk

2. *Security Risk* – risk imposed on the organization because of a third party's security practices – security risk is often related to privacy risk and workforce risk

3. *Workforce Risk* – risk imposed on the organization when it grants personnel access to its facilities or network, including desktop support, mailroom, human resources, physical security, and maintenance/janitorial

What Is Our Third-Party Exposure?

Given the potential impact of third-party risk to the organization, it is crucial to correctly catalog and manage the risk associated with each critical third party. If not already done, implement a risk management process to cover all critical third-party relationships. The steps in such a process include identifying the third party and the risks they pose, measuring and assessing those risks, implementing mitigation steps to address any process gaps, monitoring the progress of those mitigation steps, and providing a governance structure to ensure these activities are faithfully carried out throughout the term of the third party's service. The first two steps we'll call conducting a risk assessment. The CISO should be a key participant in the risk assessment. The output of the assessment should be an inventory of critical third parties that, skewing to cyber risk, includes answers to at least the following questions. Questions in bold represent data points particularly relevant to cyber risk.

- How dependent is the organization on this specific third party?
- What is the nature of the dependency? Is it operational, related to revenue? Other?
- Do they meet multiple requirements, i.e., do they have different products and services being used by multiple business units within the organization?
- Who is responsible for interacting with this third party, and who should be consulted and informed regarding the activities, controls, and risks associated with the third party?
- Is there an alternate provider in case the primary provider is no longer available?
- **What type of data and how much data are processed by this third party?**
- **Which applications does the third party use to capture, store, and process the data?**
- Is the data subject to special handling requirements?
- If this data is breached, manipulated, or lost, what is the potential impact to the organization?
- Does the third-party's location pose additional risks or obligations for your organization?
- Is the third party a regulated entity?
- If so, do the regulations pose additional risks or obligations for your organization?

Governance of Third Parties

Once the risk assessment phase is complete, organizations will typically put controls in place to secure the business processes facilitated in whole or in part by their partners. The level of these controls will be based on several factors, such as:

- The likelihood of an attack on the assets dedicated to that business process
- The impact on the business if the assets were lost or damaged
- The sensitivity of the data these assets use, process, or store

Employing a set of controls from a well-known security framework can help. But as we know, Target was PCI compliant and still got hacked. Having a framework in place is an excellent first step, but it still leaves the organization open to an enormous amount of risk involving third-party vendors, contractors, and partners. This risk is partly because we lack visibility into the third party's enterprise networks, business operations, workflows, and financial processes. All parties must remember that no matter what services an organization contracts out, responsibility and accountability still rest with the organization. We can't contract away our accountability for managing our risk.

Vendor management (often referred to as Vendor Risk Management) is now a critical part of governance, risk, and compliance (GRC) and enterprise risk management (ERM) functions in all but the smallest of organizations. Excellent vendor management practices require the insights and domain expertise of multiple parties. This includes the CISO, the legal department, IT, finance and accounting, the GRC team, departmental and business analyst teams, the executive team, and potentially the board of directors if the service under review is considered strategic.

As a general rule, the individuals requesting the service will likely have a higher risk tolerance than those charged with oversight and governance. This disparity might create tension between teams. The team that requires the service may see the vendor management and assessment process as too bureaucratic and too slow. Failing to address requirements promptly often results in non-authorized services – shadow IT or non-governed third parties. All parties need to know the business context (including issues related to internal capabilities and competencies, timing, budget, risk tolerance, and executive sponsorship) and the potential risks associated with the requested service. This context should inform the nature and extent of the diligence required for the provider.

Due Diligence

Ideally, you would capture security requirements in the RFI or RFP documentation. During the vendor diligence and assessment phase, the CISO is a critical player in evaluating the potential provider's security and privacy controls. As part of this diligence, the CISO should review the provider's audit reports, including the provider's Statement of Standards for Attestation Agreements (SSAE 18) Service Organization Controls (SOC) 1 and SOC 2 audits. These reports should assess controls through Type I (design) and Type II (operational effectiveness) testing. A report that includes only Type I testing is not sufficient. The SOC 1 report focuses on the controls related to financial reporting, and the service provider organization defines the controls. The SOC 2 report may focus on one or more of the five Trust Services Criteria: security, availability, processing integrity, confidentiality, and privacy. The controls related to each principle are prescriptive and not subject to the service provider's discretion. While these audits provide "reasonable assurance," CISOs are well-served by expanding their assessment and validation of the provider's privacy and security controls.

- Additional diligence may be in order depending upon the nature and scope of the contracted services. If the organization is sharing sensitive data with the provider (e.g.,

PII, PHI, IP, pricing data) or if the provider's services support mission-critical operations (e.g., an e-commerce site or other applications or business processes supporting the organization's operations), the lack of common certifications or control audits within your provider's domain should be a bright red flag in evaluating that provider. Revalidate annually as a lapsed certification or audit report is a definite red flag.

- We recommend site visits for critical third parties and third parties that handle highly sensitive data. It's essential to meet the team that will be providing the services delivered to the organization. Equally important, learn about the third party's hiring practices. How are applicants screened and assessed? How are certifications and skills evaluated? Are background checks performed? Look to expand your contacts within the provider's organization beyond those with a vested interest in the transaction. Use these site visits to plant the seeds and then nurture working partnerships with the third party.

- **From an operational perspective, it's essential to know about the third party's business continuity and disaster recovery planning.** The provider should have client-facing versions of these documents ready for review as part of the due diligence process. How often are the BC/DR plans tested? Are the exercises tabletop or functional cutovers of processes? What is the scope of BC/DR procedures?

For many service providers, the procedures may only address internal operations and not necessarily those of their clients. Are clients allowed or encouraged to participate in continuity planning? How does the service provider assess risk? How frequently are risk assessments conducted? More importantly, what steps do they take to remediate known risks?

- Financial due diligence is also required. Determine if the service provider is financially viable. Is the service provider profitable? If not, why not and when do they expect to become profitable? What are their key metrics and how important is your business to their profitability? What is their source of funding? Do they have audited financials available for review? Your vendors have vendors. Where practical, try incorporating these secondary and tertiary relationships into your vendor assessment efforts.

A final dimension to assess third-party partners on is how they align with the organization's strategic goals. Here are three categories to consider:

- *Strategic Partners* – The organization is highly dependent on the third party and there is a high cost (not necessarily financial) to replace them as their operations become essential to the business over time.

- *Emerging Partners* – Typically these are small to mid-size, have a specific service or solution critical to the organization, and could grow over time into a strategic partner.

- *Operational Partners* – These providers are focused on daily business operations, and they are not expensive to replace. They have earned their position by providing quality service at minimal cost to the business.

This context will inform the nature and extent of diligence that is conducted to evaluate the provider and its services. Your organization should also determine the long-term impacts of not developing certain capabilities and competencies internally. Within security, a lack of internal resources to address certain security functions may be appropriate given the organization's operating model and its security strategy, but it may also hamstring the organization should external resources be hard to find or cost prohibitive. Decisions regarding what should be managed internally versus outsourced should not be taken lightly.

Contract Management

There will be specific expectations and obligations for both parties outlined in the written contract. Contracts with strategic vendors should have board or senior management approval. The level of detail in contract provisions will depend on the level of risk and the third party's scope of services.

The requirements the organization details and captures from the RFI and RFP must be as detailed as possible and address items beyond the essential function or activity requested by a given department or line of business. A multi-disciplinary approach is necessary. Depending upon the requirements, stipulations regarding how to govern and secure non-public information (NPI), electronic protected health information (ePHI), and intellectual property (IP) may be necessary. The requirements should outline specific detail related to invoicing, metrics for invoicing, and service delivery response times.

It's critical that the master services agreement (MSA) and associated addenda with the service provider explicitly convey what is and is not covered as part of the service. It's also critical to understand and evaluate the order of precedence between various legal agreements. There may be a statement of work (SOW), proposals, addenda, and an MSA that you need to rank regarding the controlling contract, should an issue or discrepancy arise. You must declare war on ambiguity. Ensure that service demarcations between the service provider and your organization are explicit and not subject to any ambiguity.

There are real challenges in negotiating service contracts when there are asymmetries between the parties. A smaller organization negotiating a cloud service contract with Amazon's AWS or Microsoft's Azure will have almost no ability to make material changes to the provider's MSA. In many cases, these contracts give a simple "I Accept" option on a website. Corporate counsel will likely cringe when they see the terms and conditions typical with these click-through agreements. In many cases, the limitations on liability, disclaimers of warranty, and other fit-for-purpose clauses are genuinely one-sided in favor of the service provider.

These asymmetries can also occur in the opposite direction when a larger customer procures services from a smaller organization. These contracts can be so rigorous as to produce an existential risk to the service provider if they have a material breach. Equally important in these scenarios are the financial implications of required contract provisions. A large customer may mandate that its service provider submit to audits, carry cyber liability insurance, conduct vulnerability analysis and penetration testing, and have well-documented and tested BC/DR procedures, all of which come with costs. If the provider's fees do not adequately cover these requirements, its financial viability may be in jeopardy.

Provisioning and Implementation

Inspect what you expect. During the provisioning and implementation phase, it's critical to start the relationship with the service provider correctly. If there's a right to audit clause, audit their services. Ask tough questions and triangulate on the answers by asking more than one contact at the service provider the same question. Assurances are most important in this phase. Validate as many elements associated with the contract as is practicable. The provisioning and implementation phase is a high-risk period given the number of extenuating circumstances that could impact service delivery. Ensure that contracted services and deliverables are indeed provided. If these are delayed, understand the root cause for the delay and explicitly when the services will be delivered.

Risk Monitoring

There is a rule of thumb for risk monitoring that is common for managing third-party providers:

"The more critical the relationship, the more oversight and monitoring required." Management needs to allocate sufficient resources, such as qualified staff, to monitor and manage all third-party relationships.

Performance Monitoring

Verify that third-party providers are still able to perform services. Review the third party's financial condition annually, including audited financial statements and independent attestation of the third party's ability to perform services as contracted. Review the third-party provider's insurance coverage to ensure they have adequate coverage and validate that they have cyber insurance and that your organization is named as an additional insured (if/where applicable). Review the provider's financial obligations to other parties and ascertain if they are being met. Review the adequacy of and adherence to internal controls. Monitor compliance with required laws, regulations, rules, and policies. Review reports for third-party performance to ensure they meet contractual requirements, performance standards, and service level agreements. This level of diligence is clearly scaled to address strategic vendors – those that could materially impact your organization's services and obligations.

Decommissioning

We should anticipate the end of a service-provider relationship and have contractually agreed-upon procedures to handle potential scenarios. These include the migration to another service provider (effectively moving to a competitor of the service provider) and transferring data and information back to the organization or the destruction of data to agreed-upon standards. None of these activities are easy, but planning for their occurrence, despite the challenges, is required for good governance.

Concerning data transference or destruction, you must evaluate a host of technical requirements. Given how large data sets are today, bringing data back home may not be technically feasible or require months to accomplish over traditional network connections. Data destruction may also present challenges when the service provider's infrastructure is multi-tenant. "Destroying" the disks containing your data may not be feasible on shared storage arrays. For these scenarios, understanding how the service provider sanitizes its storage is a must. It may also be necessary to plan for longer-term retention periods where the underlying contract has expired.

How to Assess and Work with Vendors Post Selection

What happens when the CISO becomes engaged after the fact? This scenario is indeed quite common. When a CISO becomes engaged after contracts are executed and service delivery begins, there is still ample room to improve the process. Specifically, the CISO should seek to validate operational metrics and controls that impact the service's security. If the contracts incorporated a right to audit clause, the CISO, or a competent delegate from the CISO's team, should be part of the auditing team that evaluates the service provider's activities. This evaluation is an excellent opportunity for the CISO to liaise with the CISO at the service provider.

Equally important, if there are ongoing stewardship meetings with the provider, the CISO should participate and ask some of the tough questions related to existing practices. Should there be gaps in the provider's governance and security practices, the CISO can provide recommendations for improvement and work with legal counsel if necessary to formalize requests to remediate the issues (effectively to cure). The CISO or a designated member of the CISO's team should also be actively engaged in the incident response and breach notification procedures associated with the provider. Ideally, this engagement will foster better connections with the service provider's security team and result in the sharing of best practices.

Good vendor management practices are a must. Organizations today depend upon a diverse and growing ecosystem of vendors, service providers, and independent contractors. This ecosystem's security controls and information governance practices are effectively "in scope" for the CISO. Given organizational reliance upon third party services, assessing third-party security practices, ensuring compliance, validating security metrics, creating data-flow diagrams to understand trust boundaries, and reviewing audit reports are as much a part of the CISO's core responsibilities as internal security practices and policies.

Key Insights and Recommended Next Steps

It is vital for the business to develop relationships with its external partners so that assessments and planning become opportunities for improvement and not merely expressions of risk definition. In fact, good third-party relationships are cooperative, two-way knowledge exchanges that recognize shared risk and shared opportunities for improvement. The CISO is one of the critical team members providing governance over managing this risk. The CISO or a designated member of the CISO's team should also be actively engaged in the incident response and breach notification procedures associated with the provider.

It is essential to understand the state of your organization's vendor management program. Specifically, know who has access to your sensitive data (as well as whose data you have access to), who has access to your environment (physical and virtual), and how reliable the information security controls are at the organizations with whom you contract. To that end, having an accurate inventory of your third parties is foundational. It is extremely difficult to understand what protections you need if you don't know with whom you are sharing data. This inventory will give you a baseline of what third parties the business relies on and the data to which they have access.

Many of these vendor management program requirements and actions will be outside the CISO's realm of coverage. Still, countless external vendors will require access to corporate data and systems. This requires effective cooperation, frequent contact, educating each other on the business processes, and risk mitigation strategies. The ultimate shared goal is protecting the organization while optimizing the organization's benefit from the partnership.

This cooperative relationship, both with key third parties and management colleagues who manage the engagements, become vital to preventing the organization from making an ill-advised choice to respond to a crisis by engaging a third party in a way that could make the situation worse. A current, illustrative example would be the way in which COVID-19 vaccination status might be tracked by an organization. Third-party providers who offered services would need to protect this information with the same level of diligence as other protected health information. Poorly controlled processes put both the contracting and providing organizations at risk of regulatory sanction, and potentially exposes sensitive health information. The rollout of programs to respond to changing governmental guidance might make such a process more difficult to properly control and increase the temptation to use a trusted partner or specialist firm, making it essential for the CISO to be a trusted partner throughout the organization.

Senior management and the board should be intimately aware of the dependencies the organization places on its material third-party relationships. They should know which business units rely on the third party, who is responsible for interacting with this third party, the risks associated with the third party, and whether there is an alternate provider in case the primary provider is no longer available.

Chapter 4

Regulatory, Compliance and Audit

The farther backward you can look, the farther forward you can see.
~ Winston Churchill

Executive Summary

In most organizations, the CISO plays a significant role in compliance activities. This usually includes a combination of high-level sponsorship, guidance, control testing, program management, and direct control execution. This variability, combined with the myriad different backgrounds of CISOs, can lead to an over-reliance on using the CISO role for the organization's compliance function.

Most organizations are likely subjected to one or more regulatory compliance obligations that require appropriate security controls over sensitive data. This could be protected health information (PHI), personally identifiable information (PII), or non-public information (NPI), as well as cardholder data for those organizations that process credit card transactions. Where these obligations originate can have significant implications for how compliance is resourced, staffed, and executed, and drive wildly different consequences for lack of compliance. The potential for these consequences to subject firms to material monetary damages or sanctions that threaten the firm's competitive posture may directly require the participation or oversight of senior leadership and often the board of directors.

In our experience, the essential ingredient in good compliance and security and privacy governance is an effective and thoughtful working partnership between the CISO and the senior leadership team. The CISO will be responsible for their own key controls and provide guidance and oversight for controls executed in other departments. The CISO's peers must view the partnership and oversight as an indispensable doublecheck rather than another compliance burden. The CISO must avoid overreach and resolve control non-performance without assuming responsibility for the failed controls, as any risks discovered belong to the business and not the CISO. This should be reinforced by an effective audit program that helps the organization strictly maintain separation of duties.

Ensuring Good Compliance Outcomes

Compliance and audit responsibilities fall under the domain of Governance, Risk and Compliance, or GRC. The CISO's GRC role is typically a combination of assessment, guidance, execution, and monitoring tasks. In this chapter, we're going to start with outlining the breadth of compliance outcomes and then address a recommended approach to generating successful results. We'll finish with the role that audits play in helping the CISO and the broader organization meet compliance obligations.

Legislation Is Changing Cybersecurity

Let's look at how international, federal, and state legislation impacts cybersecurity practices and risk analyses. While many essential laws speak to security, we highlight and discuss the following based on their *cyber* impact:

Landmark Legislation with Cyber Impact[8]

- 1914 Federal Trade Commission Act (FTCA)
- 1977 Foreign Corrupt Practices Act (FCPA)
- 1999 Graham-Leach-Bliley Act (GLBA)
- 2002 Sarbanes-Oxley Act (SOX)
- 2003 California Senate Bill SB 1386
- 2009 The Health Information Technology for Economic and Clinical Health Act (HITECH)
- 2013 Protection of Personal Information Act (POPIA)
- 2018 General Data Protection Regulation (GDPR)
- 2020 California Consumer Privacy Act (CCPA)
- 2021 Personal Information Protection Law (PIPL)

---

[8] POPIA is the privacy regulation for South Africa, GDPR pertains to citizens of the European Union, PIPL is China's first comprehensive law for regulating online data and personal information. The United States contributed the rest.

The oldest act is also, perhaps, the most impactful. The Federal Trade Commission Act (FTCA[9]) that created the U.S. Federal Trade Commission (FTC) in 1914 arguably has had the most significant impact on cybersecurity practices in the U.S. Section 5 of the FTCA prohibits "unfair or deceptive acts or practices in or affecting commerce." This single phrase has done more to create a minimum set of cybersecurity practices across the economy than any other line in regulation (even the famous Section 404 of the Sarbanes-Oxley Act). The FTC has dramatically expanded its role in protecting consumers by leveraging Section 5 to require consumer-facing organizations to protect the privacy and security of non-public information.

The FTC's primary enforcement tool is the consent order. Consent orders (also referred to as consent decrees) function in practice as settlement agreements, although the respondent does not admit liability related to "alleged" practices. Consent orders frequently follow notable data breaches where the organization failed to "respect the individual's privacy and protect the individual's data." Effectively, the consumer provided their information with the expectation that their privacy would be respected, and their data protected. Having their data breached suggests an unfair and deceptive trade practice, to wit the consent order.

Interestingly enough, the 1977 Foreign Corrupt Practices Act (FCPA), enforced by the Department of Justice (DOJ) and the Securities and Exchange Commission (SEC) for public companies, indirectly lays the groundwork for the current focus on security controls. Compliance with the FCPA requires establishing an appropriate internal controls framework to prevent or detect the bribery of foreign officials or other fraudulent activities. While the

---

[9] Not to be confused with the Federal Tort Claims Act, also abbreviated FTCA, that gives private companies the right to sue the U.S. federal government for most torts committed by persons acting on behalf of the federal government.

FCPA does not reference information technology, the Act's provisions require internal controls to be in place to ensure that accounting transactions are accurate, complete, and valid. Effectively, these transaction attributes create a level of assurance that accounting procedures and practices reflect managerial authorization and preclude inappropriate financial activity, in this case, bribery. The FCPA's emphasis on a program of internal control laid the groundwork for Sarbanes-Oxley's impact on IT, where accounting practices are underpinned and supported by pervasive IT general controls.

Before turning to SOX, let's take a look at the Gramm-Leach-Bliley Act (GLBA) of 1999. GLBA, primarily enforced by the FTC, is focused on the privacy and protection of non-public information maintained by financial institutions. The FTC's consent decrees create an expectation of security practices. And the effect of GLBA is to mandate specific security requirements for the financial services industry. GLBA requires that financial services organizations – broadly defined as "significantly engaged" in financial services – comply with the security guidelines delineated in Section 501(b) of the Act.

GLBA Security Compliance Requirements

The guidelines formally establish the compliance requirements for financial services organizations to include the following:

- Establish a response program to address unauthorized access or use of customer information that could result in "substantial harm" or "inconvenience" to a customer

- Identify "reasonably" foreseeable threats (both internal and external)

- Assess the "likelihood" and "potential" of these threats

- Implement administrative, physical, and technical security controls to protect customer information

- Assess the efficacy of the overall security program

- Establish procedures to evaluate the security programs and contractual obligations of service providers

- Designate security responsibility within the organization

GLBA is significantly more prescriptive concerning IT and security practices than Sarbanes-Oxley. The Sarbanes-Oxley Act of 2002 (SOX) barely touches upon IT in the law's actual language. The role of IT with SOX is mostly by inference. SOX's focus is on the internal controls over financial reporting (ICFR) and having mechanisms in place for executive accountability, board oversight, and the independence of external auditors.

While SOX does not overtly prescribe practices such as those required by GLBA, SOX did have an essential contribution to cybersecurity. The law effectively created linkages between accounting and business processes and the underlying IT infrastructure and IT practices. Auditors expanded their review of internal controls to encompass enterprise resource planning and general ledger systems and line-of-business applications that ultimately inform or feed financial data to these accounting systems. The audit community justifiably expanded the scope of ICFR to include IT general controls (ITGC) – security being a domain in this assessment.

California's SB 1386 (passed in 2002 and placed into effect in 2003) was the first state law requiring breach notification when there is a compromise of California resident's non-public information. SB 1386 provides an exclusion for encrypted data. The bill was complemented the next year with AB 1950, which added two essential extensions to SB 1386's requirements. Specifically, AB 1950 requires "entities...to implement and maintain reasonable security procedures to protect personal information from unauthorized access, destruction, use, modification, or disclosure." AB 1950 further requires third parties processing NPI on behalf of the entity to employ similar security procedures and requires that the service contract contain these provisions. Third-party contractual obligations – effectively requiring supplier due diligence – began with GLBA. As we will see, supplier security standards continue with HIPAA-HITECH in the form of business associate agreements (BAAs). There are also significant expectations of vendor risk assessment and prescriptive controls outlined in the GDPR (notably related to cross border data transfers and required security controls between controllers and processors).

Collectively, the culmination of HIPAA-HITECH requirements is driving many necessary security reforms in IT. The impact of HIPAA-HITECH on IT practices, and security and privacy specifically, is similar to the effect of SOX on IT, despite SOX's relatively limited legal requirements for IT and security. While the impacts of both laws on IT and security practices are profound, HIPAA-HITECH shares more common prescriptive elements with GLBA. HIPAA-HITECH requires organizations that store, process, or otherwise use protected health information (PHI), including electronic forms of PHI (ePHI), to implement prescriptive practices spanning administrative, technical, and physical controls. HIPAA-HITECH requirements incorporate both "required" and "addressable" controls that have some nuance related to the size, risk, and complexity of the environment at hand.

The Fundamental Requirements of HIPAA-HITECH

Administrative Safeguards: Security Management Processes (risk analyses, risk management, system review, and sanction policies) are all considered required activities. There is also a requirement to assign security responsibility and conduct incident management and contingency planning. Critically, the regulation requires that business associate agreements with service providers that store, process, or otherwise use PHI or ePHI on behalf of a covered entity or another business associate codify security and privacy controls. CFR 164.308 highlights the required and addressable administrative safeguards mandated by HIPAA-HITECH. These boil down to security and privacy governance and a requirement for a designated individual within the organization to establish and be accountable for mandated security programs. CFR 164.308 covers requisite administrative controls.

Physical Safeguards: The required and addressable controls related to physical safeguards encompass workstation security, controls over physical media (including disposal), and facility access. CFR 164.310 covers requisite physical controls.

Technical Safeguards: The required controls related to technical safeguards can be quite challenging where there are "emergency access" procedures that potentially override other requirements. Availability of systems in healthcare, for example, can be a life-and-death matter and therefore outweighs the important confidentiality and integrity security objectives. The necessary balancing act between these three attributes highlights the inherent conflict between confidentiality and integrity (which require potentially performance-impacting controls) and availability. The technical safeguards of HIPAA-HITECH incorporate audit controls, access controls (including unique user identification – required for non-repudiation), and authentication procedures. CFR 164.312 covers requisite technical controls.

General Data Protection Regulation (GDPR)

The European Union's GDPR has global reach and pervasive impacts on privacy and security practices. While several articles within the GDPR are significant, including the infamous Article 17 (the right to erasure or "right to be forgotten"), there is one article in particular that establishes an important threshold for security practices – Article 25, which calls for "data protection by design and by default."

The GDPR presupposes that organizations maintain a level of visibility and organizational knowledge about the data they collect, process, share with third parties, and store as part of their operations. Article 25's "by design and by default" clause requires that organizations implement data protection with techniques and technology such as pseudonymization. Importantly, it also requires data minimization practices. There is an explicit requirement that organizations only collect the minimum information necessary to fulfill the processing activities' stated purpose. The routine overcollection of personal data that many organizations practice is clearly in data protection authorities' crosshairs. Like SOX and process narratives, Article 30 of the GDPR requires a detailed record of processing activities, including a description of the "technical and organizational security measures" employed. Article 32 outlines the security expectations for personal data processing, including the pseudonymization or encryption of personal data and procedures to assess security controls' effectiveness.

Like the critical precedent established with California's SB 1386, Article 33 of the GDPR requires that organizations that have experienced a data breach notify the applicable data protection authority within 72 hours after becoming aware of the breach. Beyond these highlighted articles, the GDPR requires comprehensive, documented, and ingrained privacy and security practices for in-scope organizations.

The California Consumer Privacy Act (CCPA) is frequently described as the California equivalent to the GDPR, but this comparison minimizes essential distinctions between the CCPA and the GDPR. The CCPA, unlike the GDPR, requires that organizations notify consumers regarding the categories and sources of personal information that the organization collects from the consumer and whether this information is sold to a third party. Consumers can opt-out of having their information sold to third parties.

Similar to the privacy rights established in Chapter III of the GDPR, consumers are afforded new rights with the CCPA, including the right to access and correct the information collected about them, the right to preclude their information from being sold, the right to have their data deleted (there are obviously caveats on when and where this is applicable, similar to the GDPR's Article 17), the right of private action to sue organizations that fail to secure their data adequately, and the right to non-discrimination when consumers exercises their rights. Organizations should consider the rights established in Chapter III of the GDPR and the specific rights noted in the CCPA as setting the tone for future privacy regulation. Organizations that currently aren't required to abide by these practices will likely find that their privacy and security practices will eventually be subject to some form of similar regulatory oversight.

Analogous to the GDPR's Articles 25 and 32, the CCPA establishes an explicit expectation of reasonable security (§1798.150). Unlike the GDPR, the CCPA does not offer guidance on what security measures are considered reasonable. However, the 2016 California Data Breach Report, authored by the State Attorney General, is prescriptive, providing a definition of reasonable security that includes adopting a security framework or standard. The "Critical Security Controls" provided by the Center for Internet Security is offered as an acceptable framework. The use of multi-factor authentication (MFA) for systems containing personal information and encryption, notably for portable devices, is included in the framework.

Collectively, the GDPR and the CCPA have had the effect of focusing executive attention on privacy and requisite security controls over the data that organizations collect on data subjects or consumers. Importantly, both regulations require that organizations have a more in-depth knowledge of their data processing activities and the controls over these activities, including data flows. For CISOs, this knowledge facilitates the implementation and management of security controls that are more closely aligned to in-scope regulations.

Common Threads of a Cybersecurity Program

Most information security organizations, as they mature, start designating individuals with more focused duties. One of the first positions to receive this treatment is the dedicated security compliance role. Larger organizations typically call this "Governance" or "Security Governance."

In many organizations, Governance initially applies only to compliance activities and does not address program effectiveness or performance management. However, it usually does include being both a subject matter expert (SME) in the security compliance role and acting in a follow-up or "Project Management" capacity to ensure other departments within the organization understand and follow through on their information security compliance duties.

One unpleasant fact of security compliance is that requirements tend to expand over time. A frequent contributor to this expanding security compliance burden is that auditors and regulators hold controls testing and demonstrating compliance to ever-higher standards. Auditors and regulators are becoming more educated about the risks they assess and are better trained in the tools and methods for conducting those assessments.

As we have noted, a combination of international, federal, and state legislation is changing the cybersecurity landscape. Clearly, with so many overlapping standards, frameworks, and legal obligations facing organizations today, it can be confusing for the board and executive management (let alone CISOs) to determine where to begin. There are some essential common threads that we can derive from the review above that will provide clear guidance on where to start. Specifically, every organization should, at a minimum, have the following:

- A designated security officer – It's critical that someone within the organization assume responsibility and advocate for good security practices. GLBA requires a designated security officer, as do various state breach notification laws and HIPAA-HITECH.

- A program to evaluate and assess risk – Ultimately, cyber risk is a subset of overall enterprise risk management (ERM). Organizations need to foment ERM practices and look at risk beyond traditional financial perspectives. Assessing cyber risk is an essential organizational competency. This program must also be applied to mergers, acquisitions and divestitures. Shocks to control execution because of inadequate due diligence can potentially lead to a material weakness for financial statements or a qualified opinion on a SOC 2 report.

- Data classification – Organizations need to know what types of information they collect, process, and share with customers, vendors, service providers, and affiliates. Data flow diagrams (discussed later in this book) are an essential tool for gaining this understanding. Knowing the categories and sources of information collected about consumers is an explicit requirement of the CCPA.

- Vendor due diligence – No organization operates in isolation. Organizations rely on service providers that complement and extend the organization's capabilities. Assessing third-party cyber risk, security capabilities, and mandated security practices should be part of standard vendor due diligence. It's imperative to know where and how third parties impact cybersecurity for the organization. This third-party evaluation is mandated by GLBA, HIPAA-HITECH, GDPR, and California's breach notification laws, among other regulations.

- Executive responsibility for internal controls (including security controls) – What is clear from SOX and the FCPA is that executive management is responsible for establishing the tone at the top and, more concretely, documenting and testing internal controls.

- The board of directors should take responsibility for providing oversight of cyber risk management. Boards have a fiduciary duty to evaluate the overall risk appetites of the organizations they oversee. Boards need to understand their organizations' cyber risk profiles and the impact of risk on strategic business operations.

State and federal regulations, coupled with industry and sector frameworks, are removing the ambiguity or mystery associated with security functions. The result is greater clarity regarding the minimum cybersecurity practices that every organization should employ.

Build Compliance into Your Program

Most recommended controls for compliance requirements promote basic cybersecurity common sense. The right framework is critical. You use it as a baseline for evaluating the effectiveness of the organization's cybersecurity risk management program. A framework such as ISO 27001 or NIST Cybersecurity Framework (NIST CSF) is a good start. Either framework would provide a structure that your organization, its regulators, and its partners can use to create, assess, or improve their current risk management programs.

We recommend the NIST Cybersecurity Framework. It is designed to address how an organization securely processes information. This framework has five core functions: _Identify_, _Protect_, _Detect_, _Respond_, and _Recover_. This framework provides the option of implementing it in tiers, from Tier 1, "Partial," to Tier 4, "Adaptive." Implementation depends on the organization's risk appetite and how rigorously the business wants to incorporate cybersecurity risk management practices. This picture demonstrates the flow of information and decisions required to implement the NIST Cybersecurity Framework.

This framework also contains an annex which lists all applicable security controls. This annex lists the individual controls under each of the five core functions and provides cross-references between the individual controls and other risk management frameworks, which may be required depending on the industry of the organization.

How to Engage with Your Auditors

The last topic for this chapter is how to engage auditors and regulators. It is imperative to recognize the role that auditors and regulators play.

Broadly speaking, there are four types of functions involved:

- Internal Audit is a function commissioned by the board of directors to help the board understand how management addresses specific types of risk.

- External Audit is a function also commissioned by the board of directors, in this case to provide an independent third-party assessment. CPA firms, including the "Big 4" multinational firms and other regional firms, usually carry out these audits. Results are typically reported directly to the board of directors. Examples include SSAE 18 SOC 1 and SOC 2 audits.

- Similar to, but distinct from, external audit are third-party attestation firms that perform specialized compliance tests, such as adhering to PCI-DSS.

- Finally, regulatory bodies, such as the FFIEC, deploy examiners to review an organization's compliance with its statutory obligations. In many cases, regulators also rely on reports from independent auditors who assess the subject organization's compliance using an agreed-upon test for compliance.

These relationships are all built on timeliness and transparency, which builds trust. Organizations get the best audit results (not necessarily the lowest number of findings) when they engage auditors as partners.

The board empowers internal audit to help them provide effective oversight. Because of the rapid and wealth-destroying ramp up in cybercrime, boards of directors are demanding full assessments by their audit teams of where their organizations stand on cyber preparedness, including regarding the risks of ransomware. The board must have a comprehensive view of the organization's risk profile. These audits also provide an excellent opportunity to increase management attention on cyber initiatives and keep the board informed.

The board also engages external auditors, and these groups are another tool for the board to provide oversight. As of October 2011, public companies are expected to address potentially material cybersecurity risks and cyber incidents in the Management's Discussion and Analysis of Financial Condition and Results of Operations (MD&A) that they file with the SEC every quarter. The SEC expanded upon this guidance in February 2018 with additional expectations for cybersecurity risk disclosures.

Third-party assessors for contractual obligations like PCI-DSS validate your assertion that you comply with the controls you agreed to take on, for instance, when you contracted with a member of the Payment Card Industry, such as a bank, merchant service, or payment gateway. While they do have a business reason to demonstrate independence and integrity in the standards body's eyes to maintain their accredited status, they are hired by and are working for your organization. Management should approach the relationship as a partnership. Where controls are weak, work with the assessor to design compensating controls, and a path to strong controls. They don't want to see you fail.

Examiners for regulatory bodies are different in that your organization does not employ them or hire them through any contract with your organization. However, they typically share a fundamental desire to see you succeed. Their job is to protect the systemic integrity of the industry they regulate. Given this responsibility, they can sanction your organization directly, which can mean civil and criminal penalties, orders to cease operations, and orders to address issues within mandated timeframes. Though the consequences can be severe, the engagement model is similar. Setting the scope is essential. For example, it's not helpful to have non-regulated lines of business examined by regulators. It wastes their time and your time and creates confusion and potential inappropriate jeopardy.

In general, employees don't need to be "coached" to work with auditors. Being straightforward and transparent about work processes and the ability to document assertions is the best approach. What does help is to prepare employees so that they know what to expect from their audit partners and what management expects of them.

It's important to remember that auditors are subject matter experts first in the audit or examination process; second, sometimes to a much lesser extent, in the business process they are assessing; and then third, especially if they are not employees of your company, in the knowledge of how your internal processes work and the relationships between internal parties. Additionally, auditors may not have the same level of technical depth on specific security techniques and controls. To avoid confusion, especially where compensating or mitigating controls are used, security leaders should validate the auditor's understanding and agreement that this approach meets audit requirements and the spirit of the regulation being assessed.

Fixing the Relationship with Your Auditor

As we mentioned above, these are trust relationships built on timeliness and transparency. We have listened to and overheard a lot of skepticism, distrust, and outright fear from individual contributors to senior executives about interacting with auditors. Some are worried they will get in trouble for doing something wrong. Many people view the time spent with auditors as wasted time and the time spent gathering evidence and providing documentation as busywork. This viewpoint causes behaviors that, purposely or not, obstruct the assessment process.

In some cases, the auditors are assigned "handlers" to choreograph the activity. Process owners are coached to provide guarded answers and escalate every question for which they don't have a prepared response. We have also seen the opposite case where inexperienced auditors bring poor time management skills, poorly thought-out evidence requests, and negative, accusatory attitudes to audits, putting everyone on guard.

This obstruction causes distrust and adds stress. The distrust comes from the reasonable belief that team members are trying to hide something they are uncomfortable exposing or that minor failures will be misinterpreted or used to justify punitive remedies. The stress arises because the audits are scoped for specific resources (on both sides) within a certain timeframe, with competing deadlines looming.

As you can imagine, distrust and stress often create a dysfunctional working relationship. Requests for documentation start getting escalated. Escalated or not, documentation is hurriedly assembled and is often incorrect or incomplete. As operational requirements take more time from participants, "just get it done" replaces "do it right." At some point in this dysfunctional downward spiral, "do whatever the auditor says to get this over" becomes the unspoken (and sometimes spoken) strategy to end the pain. The result puts auditors in the position of forsaking their independence, and process owners are forced to abandon their duty to perform the process in the way they believe yields the best results. Under these circumstances, management receives much less value from the audit, and the board rarely gets an accurate understanding of the state of the business. With these poor results, catastrophe lurks around the corner.

So how do we fix this? Building the required trust starts well before the audit fieldwork begins. Management and the auditors need to invest the time to agree on scope, objectives, roles, and responsibilities. It's crucial at this stage to surface issues that otherwise will cause problems later. For instance, does the auditor have experience with the organization that suggests that timeliness will be a problem? Has management had experience with the auditor in the past that suggests they will make numerous poorly targeted requests due to a lack of understanding about the organization's environment? Both of these problems are quite common, and both are addressable.

By treating your auditors as partners and prioritizing building a mutually trusting relationship founded on timeliness and transparency principles, the audit process can be a valuable tool for keeping the organization's information systems and data secure and focusing management attention where it is most needed.

One final thought on the audit process: the auditor is not a whistleblower hotline. Gently remind your employees that they should bring internal issues to a neutral member of the management team, the legal organization, Human Resources, or another appropriate person.

Key Insights and Recommended Next Steps

Driven by governments and partners, the modern corporation must deal effectively with overlapping regulations meant to safeguard data. Rather than deal with each mandate as a one-off, a better approach is to, at a minimum, centralize oversight, and if possible, drive consistency in control execution across the organization.

The CISO's role supporting the regulatory, compliance, and audit requirements of the organization includes a mix of controls to perform, controls to assess, controls to monitor, and controls to guide. The CISO might own the compliance program but cannot own all control performance. Management must share ownership of controls relevant to their organization. It is critical that the audit function assist the board with maintaining appropriate separation of duties for effective control oversight. This partnership between process owners (own and manage), the CISO (oversight), and the audit function (independent assurance) forms the "three lines of defense."[10]

Senior management and the board of directors need to work with the CISO to create and maintain an audit program that gives management and the board visibility into operational effectiveness as well as control weaknesses and blind spots where risk lurks. The board must require a comprehensive view of the organization's risk profile, including cyber preparedness, and the risks associated with the proliferation of ransomware. While accountability within the senior leadership team is critical, absent potential malfeasance or a pattern of lack of ownership or lack of vision, outcomes from audit activity should tilt toward improvement and away from recrimination.

---

[10] *Three Lines of Defense*, Alijoyo https://www2.erm-academy.org/publication/risk-management-article/three-lines-defense/

Chapter 5

Data Governance and Security Policy

No large, global, heterogeneous, multi-business- and product-line enterprise can ever hope to clean up all of its data – it's always a continuous journey. The key is knowing what data sources feed your BI applications and how confident you are about the accuracy of data coming from each source.

~ Boris Evelson, Forrester Research analyst

Executive Summary

There are few topics more critical in cybersecurity than establishing proper data governance, informed by data classification, and codified through data governance and cybersecurity (data protection) policies. For many organizations, data and information are the most valuable (strategic) assets. It is critical to align data classification and governance activities with the organization's risk management practices and, ultimately, its risk appetite.

Data classification influences the three central tenants of security: confidentiality, integrity, and availability (CIA). While each of the three tenets is important, their respective values vary from industry to industry. Data classification is also critical in prioritization because we cannot protect all data equally. A crucial part of the CISO's role is understanding which data are most important to the organization.

Policies are the foundation that underpin a security program. They explain requirements for specific processes, including who has the responsibility for process execution and the resources required for mature operations. They impact the organization's ability to defend itself against cybercriminals and recover from a cyber incident. It is the CISO and executive management's responsibility to have the correct and sufficient policies in place, ensure the organization follows these policies, and periodically update them as the business, technology, or regulatory environment changes.

It is crucial to maintain the connection between business objectives and the organization's policies. Policies have a purpose; they are written for action and inform the expectations and responsibilities of data governance. Data governance practices, when informed by explicit classification and coupled with policy that guides security functions, are integral to your security program.

What Data Is Important to Us and Where Is it?

A primary concern of information security is protecting sensitive data. One key reason organizations fail at this is that they try to protect all data equally, and their efforts collapse under the cumulative burden. The critical question for the CISO is to determine the subset of data that they should be concerned with protecting. Knowing this is critical to having a focused and successful information security program.

When we boil it down, the essential focus of data protection centers on maintaining privacy, securing financial transactions, protecting intellectual property, and safeguarding operational data. Regardless of the specific data elements involved, we are responsible for the confidentiality, integrity, and availability (CIA) of the data. Ensuring confidentiality requires proper rights to access data, integrity requires securing the data in an unaltered and accurate state, and availability requires ensuring that the data is accessible when needed. To have data security, each of these attributes must be present.

Information is fluid within, and more importantly, outside of an organization. It's not uncommon, for example, for organizations to outsource payroll services to third-party processing organizations. Payroll data includes personally identifiable information (PII), including the employees' social security numbers (SSNs), salaries, dates of birth, dependent data, and home addresses. That same organization may also outsource portions of its accounting function. The accounting firm would have access to sensitive financial information, including profit and loss detail, the value of assets, and the particulars about significant transactions.

The organization may leverage external legal counsel to file patent applications, handle merger and acquisition (M&A) activities, and work on other highly sensitive projects. A third-party marketing application might send emails or texts to clients and prospective clients containing personally identifiable information (the recipients' name and email address). Independent contractors may provide support on critical projects with access to material non-public information (MNPI). The organization may outsource manufacturing to a contract manufacturer in another country. The manufacturer could be using patented processes or other intellectual property of the organization. An external DevOps team may be helping with application development and might have real production data to test functionality.

The organization's applications might reside in multiple locations across several states and countries. Some applications and data are "in the cloud," and many lines of business, given the capacity challenges with traditional IT, use SaaS services to meet some of their requirements. Employees have personal mobile phones that they use to receive email and texts messages outside of the office. These messages may include attachments containing any number of data elements, be they sensitive employee records, sales and prospecting activity, or confidential strategy and initiative detail of the firm. Employees also bring their own devices to work and take these devices and any company-issued laptops and mobile phones home with them when they leave the office each day. Employees use third-party file-sharing tools, personal email accounts, and external media to store information. Suffice it to say that the average organization does not know where its critical data and information are and, equally important, how they are protected, if at all, outside the organization. This is a pervasive challenge for organizations large and small.

All of these challenges are fundamentally the same for third parties providing outsourced services. They, too, have third parties helping with their core functions. Payroll processing companies may outsource application development and use third-party data centers. Staff turnover, background checks, and other controls are likely to differ from firm to firm. The number of variables impacting the location of and controls over information has grown beyond most organizations' capacity to handle them securely.

Organizations typically believe they understand what data and information they have within their enterprise boundaries. Many organizations will have standard policies in place for archiving data, along with backup schemes and disaster recovery plans. They believe this will ensure that "critical" data is always available for ongoing business operations. But is that enough? For an organization to use its data as a strategic asset, it must understand data classification and have gone through organizing and classifying its critical data and capturing the data's location, system of record used for its process, and key stakeholders who access this information.

The CISO should be working with IT leadership, privacy leadership, and department leaders, while triangulating known data stores against contracts, third-party agreements, compliance activities, and audit functions to ensure that all sensitive data sets are accounted for and receive the appropriate data governance attention.

Data Classification, Often Neglected

When a new CISO starts their job, they go through a transition process. Part of that process is to meet stakeholders from the various business units and functional groups of their company. In these meetings, the CISO can learn what is relevant to these stakeholders, their problems, and what services they believe are critical for their respective departments.

During this period, the CISO should begin to inventory the networks, applications, and data assets of their organization. They might review previous audit and assessment reports and begin to evaluate the existing cybersecurity policies. As they learn more about the organization, its compliance requirements, and its strategic goals, the data collected from these initial meetings with stakeholders will provide critical insight into projects and policies necessary to protect the company. This information also highlights the types of data and information critical for organizational success. It provides a more in-depth understanding of the data lifecycle, including creating, accessing, processing, archiving, and later, decommissioning.

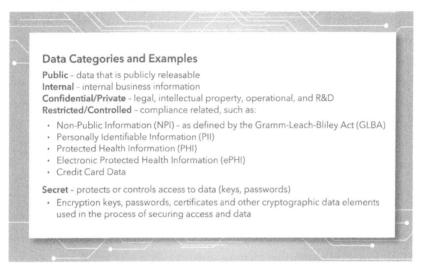

Figure 5.1 Data Categories and Examples

While it is almost self-evident that information is the lifeblood of our modern economy, how companies handle data and information suggests that we often mistreat and neglect this valuable asset. Regulatory authorities in the United States, such as the Federal Trade Commission (FTC) and contractual obligations mandated by laws such as HIPAA-HITECH's Business Associates Agreements, require organizations to know what types of data they have, who has access to this information, and how it is governed and protected. Moreover, privacy regulations such as the California Privacy Rights Act (an amended version of the California Consumer Privacy Act that goes into effect in 2023) requires organizations to explicitly know what data they collect from consumers, the sources and types of this data, and whether it is sold or transferred to other organizations. This level of detail requires that the organization has a functional data governance program.

Determining the value of this information and the associated and commensurate security and governance practices is a process that requires the CISO to be fully engaged with colleagues across the organization ... certainly beyond their traditional IT counterparts. Valued participants in this assessment include other C-level executives, corporate counsel, line-of-business executives, and the board. Also included in this group are business partners, vendors, and, potentially, regulatory authorities who may have legally mandated expectations regarding how the organization manages certain types of information.

What We Should Know About Our Data

- Data classification, location, and ownership
- Amount of data being generated, transmitted, and stored
- Data rights management, retention and destruction requirements
- Data residency requirements
- Data protection responsibilities

Figure 5.2 Key Data Attributes to Capture

Not All Data Are Created Equal

We rely on accurate, complete, timely, and valid information to make business and personal decisions. Not all data are created equal and devoting resources to protecting information with little intrinsic value is at best a distraction. This data inequality is why it is so important that organizations classify their data and information. But we also need to avoid the fundamental mistake that many organizations make, which is to try to classify every piece of data they possess. Over-classification often leads to labyrinthine data classification policies that no one follows and high costs to maintain a program that provides little value.

In addition to classifying valuable data sets, data classification efforts should also establish two policies for the organization:

Data Classification Policy – The data classification policy lists the data classification types, establishes the need for data classification to be prioritized, and provides the necessary information for business units to make decisions about their data. Data classification can be driven by the CISO or a senior IT leader but must include input from the CISO and legal counsel given the security and regulator impact of improperly classified data.

Data Handling Policy – The data handling policy should list specific requirements for handling sensitive data. Some data comes with specific training, processing, storage, and decommissioning obligations. Additionally, the data handling policy will list roles and responsibilities for personnel who interact with restricted data.

We view governing data as an organizational responsibility. Smart companies seeking competitive advantage will leverage data governance programs to add value to their revenue streams. Companies want to know what is happening across their organizations, with their vendors, their partners, and their customers. With a mature data governance program, companies can gain real-time access to their data. They will know its location and use and understand its strategic worth, and they will know the risks and costs to the organization if it is unavailable.

Policy Is Foundational

What do we mean by foundational? Information security policies provide direction on behavior in the realm of handling sensitive or protected data. This behavior might tell individuals which specific precautions they must take, inform internal developers about minimum coding requirements, or provide direction for the required level of encryption when programmatically handling data that falls within data handling requirements for regulatory or contractual obligations the organization might have. And while the high-level outcome might be the same (for example, to handle specific data in a particular way), the audience (for example, all employees, application developers, or data custodians) and detailed guidance could be very different.

There are many ways to provide guidance at different levels of detail and in various settings. These include guidelines, best practices, procedures, processes, standards, specifications, and policies.

Unintended Consequences

While information security policies serve many purposes, it's important not to overload policies to include guidelines, best practices, procedures, processes, standards, and specifications. Doing so can have several unintended negative consequences.

One unintended negative consequence is an overly restrictive development or operational environment. Procedures and standards are by nature more detailed than policy. A policy is directional, laying out high-level parameters such as establishing a requirement for stepped up or more restrictive authentication mechanisms for determining access rights for handling data at a particular sensitivity level to meet a regulatory or contractual obligation. A policy is typically drafted, recommended, and approved according to governance rules that tie publication and adoption directly to senior management or the board of directors.

Standards are measures or models. The standard might indicate that one-time password (OTP) tokens or the use of SMS are acceptable, provided passwords rotate no less than every sixty seconds, or SMS codes are valid for at most 120 seconds. Standards are typically drafted, recommended, and approved according to rules imposed by architectural groups within the organization or an external governing body.

It would be a mistake to build the standard into the policy. The group developing the standard is usually closer to operations and is more intimately familiar with operational goals, problems, and limitations.

Another unintended negative consequence is that, as noted above, auditors often test policies as part of the audit process. Investigators regularly review policies as part of investigations associated with regulatory enforcement, contract enforcement, breach investigation, whistleblower investigation, or other corporate governance-related reasons. There is often a tendency to interpret findings of failure to follow internal policy as indicative of systemic wrongdoing, lax oversight, or careless behavior.

The Exception that Proves the Rule

Data handling policies, when tied to regulatory frameworks such as HIPAA-HITECH, Sarbanes-Oxley, the European Union's GDPR, or complying with PCI-DSS, may require more explicit and prescribed policies. In those cases, the audit testing procedures specifically require verification that the organization's information security policies conform to minimum standards in domains such as cryptographic services, data retention practices, access controls, and firewall rules, among others. In these scenarios, the policies must mirror the explicit requirements of the regulations at hand.

There are also examples where regulations do not give minimum guidance, but adherence to policy might still be a specific audit topic. This condition is especially true for financial institutions, which may have a Statement on Standards for Attestation Engagements (SSAE) 18 in place for specific services they provide for their customers. It is extremely common to audit adherence to an organization's own internal security policy as part of the test of internal controls' effectiveness. Because of these requirements, some organizations fall into the trap of asking the auditors or the Qualified Security Assessor

(QSA), as in the case of PCI environments, to "just tell us what the policy is supposed to say."

However, abdicating responsibility in this manner separates decision-makers in the organization from policy setting, and that has the immediate effect of disconnecting execution from principles. Further, "the auditor told us to do it" does not help anyone understand why a policy is written one way and not another. This creates a hesitancy to make needed changes because people lack the backstory and don't know what other problems changes might cause.

Policy Has a Purpose

When we think about what we want to get from setting and publishing policy, we should focus on two fundamental things: risk mitigation and education and awareness.

As we identify risks and obligations, we set policies for the behavior we believe will allow us to manage those risks and obligations. The policy helps us draw a direct line from senior management, with whom the identification and management of these risks and obligations sit, to every line employee who carries out the wishes of management to the customer's or shareholder's benefit. This direct line also serves as an educational vehicle to inform all employees and state publicly for customers, auditors, and shareholders how the organization discharges its responsibilities.

Key Insights and Recommended Next Steps

As we stated at the beginning of this chapter, when we strip it down to the essential elements, we are concerned with maintaining privacy, securing financial transactions, protecting intellectual property, and safeguarding operational and personal data. To be effective in these objectives, we must first recognize that not all data are created equal. Knowing what types of data you have and the sensitivity of that data are critical to your ability to focus your attention and limited resources in the right way. Data classification and categorization is, therefore, essential to successful prioritization. While this process is often driven by the CISO, the privacy function, and corporate counsel, the lines-of-business should also be fully engaged.

We must also recognize that specific types of data come with specific legal requirements. For most organizations this includes, at a minimum, personally identifiable information, protected health information, and credit card or bank information. Given the velocity of data protection legislation and regulation toward increasing the rights of data subjects, the senior leadership team should work with the CISO and data privacy leader to understand their data protection obligations and validate that their functions treat the data in their charge consistent with these obligations.

To provide the proper data governance, an organization's security policy functions as a foundational control, setting the tone for its security program and data governance practices. Security policies can also become a focal point for both audit and regulatory review. Consequently, we should recognize that policy comes with liability at the audit, regulatory, and prosecutorial level when not followed, so review and adjust your policies with this in mind.

Finally, don't blur the lines between policy and procedure. Policies set the tone at the top and establish organizational expectations. Procedures define operational activities – they explain how you are going to execute what is defined in your policy.

Additional Information

Here are some of the key policies that every organization should consider incorporating into their master security policy.

Entity-Level Policies

Acceptable Use – An "Acceptable Use Policy" (AUP) needs to convey in no uncertain terms that the use of the organization's assets, including laptops, phone systems, servers, applications, networks, etc., is only for official organizational purposes. AUPs will also clearly state which behavior is prohibited by the organization. The AUP is also used to spell out the requirements for using the organization's email system, including unacceptable use of the email system, such as spam, political activities, sending inappropriate content or automatically forwarding business email outside the organization to personal email accounts.

Application Access – Within the master security policy, there should be a section that speaks to application access and associated controls. This section should overtly reference the acceptable use policy and state that access to the organization's applications is for official use only and that access rights reflect a least-privilege methodology. Application access policies will further stipulate the use of certain authentication controls based on the nature of the application at hand and the credentials and role of the individual. The policy should also capture the organization's requirement to log access attempts.

Change Management – Use an IT Service Management (ITSM) approach to look at change management practices holistically, incorporating configuration management and risk management into the change management function. This policy should indicate who is authorized to approve changes, the request process, how to triage change requests for risk, including privacy and security risks, what the rollback procedures would be should the change fail, notification procedures, and expectations related to documenting changes to configuration items (CIs) or high-level infrastructure.

Data Classification and Governance – The objective of this policy is to establish the specific requirements related to defined data sets in such a manner that there is no ambiguity regarding how to handle this data, who has access to the data and for which purposes, and how, if at all, it is to be shared with vendors, clients, and other third parties. Where data is subject to specific regulatory context, it is advisable to include an explicit reference to the regulation.

Cryptographic Services – Data classification and privacy practices will inform when and where encryption should be leveraged to protect the organization's information. The encryption policy should include procedures related to key management, key rotation, and key storage.

Incident Management – The incident management policy (and plan) is critical. The policy should have clearly defined response times and escalation procedures indicating who should be notified and by when. The procedures related to incident management should also be thoroughly documented, including how to best maintain forensic evidence.

Physical Access – Access to the organization's facilities, especially critical operational rooms, computer rooms, and data center locations, and areas where the organization maintains sensitive information, should be locked and access granted only to those individuals with a documented justification for that access. This policy should also outline expectations for logging on-site visitors and deliveries.

Vendor Management – The vendor management policy should include authorization approvals to contract third-party services, how to categorize vendor risk, legal review practices for vendor or organization-supplied contracts, expectations of a right to audit clause, data flow documentation to show which information is shared with the vendor, how such data is expected to be protected, and standards for vendor operational reviews.

Policy and Guidance for Technical Controls

While it is essential to avoid codifying procedures and best practices in policy, there are several technical policies that are so wide-spread and therefore expected that a failure to codify and implement them can subject organizations to a finding that they have not provided "due care" should investigations be required to address cyber incidents. We list the most common of these policies here.

Password Policy – Password policies should address password length and complexity (numbers, symbols, and spaces), the prohibition of using common names or other items that would make a dictionary attack easier, password aging, as well as overt prohibitions on sharing passwords.

Bring Your Own Device (BYOD) – BYOD has significant procedural challenges, including enforcement of passwords, patching, and encryption practices as well as the use of non-sanctioned applications.

Workstation Security – Depending on the organization's work environment, statutes (notably in healthcare) may require specific policies for workspace security. These policies may also be referred to as clean desk or clean workspace policies. Also, a workspace policy should have standards related to user system timeouts, physical documents containing PII and ePHI at the workspace, and other controls such as deploying anti-malware on the workstation.

Remote-Access Policy – Defines the standards for connecting to the organization's network from any host or network external to the organization. Also provides requirements for the security of any remote access technologies, for example the use of IP Security (IPsec) or Layer 2 Tunneling Protocol (L2TP) for VPN connections to the organization's network, or the implementation and use of a secure access service edge (SASE).

User Education and Awareness Policy – Specifies that employees must be trained on the organization's information security policies and practices. Awareness training policies may also call out requisite regulatory training (e.g., as required with HIPAA-HITECH).

Social Media Policy – Addresses how employees may use social media for company business and details when the use of social media on company IT assets is considered inappropriate.

Chapter 6

Measurement and Reporting

However beautiful the strategy, you should occasionally look at the results.

~Winston Churchill

Executive Summary

It is critical that the organization has reliable information upon which to base its decisions for investing the time, attention, and money needed to achieve its cybersecurity objectives. In many organizations the CISO's role is still maturing and nowhere is the journey more visible than in learning how to speak the language of business, especially regarding measuring the performance of the security team and the preparedness of the organization to protect against, detect, respond to, and recover from business disruptions.

A best practice we advocate is for the CISO to drive a collaborative metrics program, one that is based on principles that define the purpose of the program, offers guidance for the types of metrics collected, and grounds the metrics in the language of the business. The metrics program should offer coverage across the areas where the CISO provides internal and external validation for IT health, address entity-level controls required for governance over security, regulatory, and third-party risk, and provide management with the key data points to drive changes in behavior across the entire enterprise.

The final measure of success is the strategic focus of the CISO. Recognizing the high percentage of successful attacks that start by compromising the legitimate credentials of employees, the primary focus over the near future for the successful CISO should be on enlisting and empowering all employees to contribute to the cyber health of the company. After assuring themselves that they have the control coverage and technology footprint required, that they have documented their business processes, and that operational resiliency and risk management are essential value-add contributions to the enterprise, successful CISOs will be improving employee education and enhancing their communications and collaboration capabilities so that they can drive systemic change throughout the organization.

The Fundamentals of a Metrics Program

Peter Drucker's famous quote, "If you can't measure it, you can't manage it," is used so often it is now a cliché. The modern corporation has its origin in operationalizing and improving the efficiency and effectiveness of manufacturing goods. Through continual improvement driven by measurement and reporting, we can reduce process time, improve quality, and reduce cost.

We design manufacturing processes with the need to measure their efficiency and effectiveness in mind. This discipline also appears in the design and creation of computer code, such that best practice is to develop quality assurance (QA) test scripts in conjunction with the actual code, rather than as an afterthought once applications or modules have been deployed. The advent of agile development methodologies has given rise to DevOps and DevSecOps teams that locate the continual testing of the effectiveness of code and system configurations, along with vulnerability scanning and other security tests, as close as possible to both the development process and the developer community. And of course, measuring uptime, throughput, load, and the presence of known security vulnerabilities are de rigueur in the modern data center, and remain an area of continued focus as companies migrate their applications to the cloud.

It is essential to have a clear understanding of the goals and objectives for both the organization and the metrics and reporting program. This understanding is essential because as the CISO communicates progress within their team, to their peers and senior leadership, and to the board of directors, each audience is going to need a frame of reference. Each audience needs to know the objective, the current behaviors, and the change in status over time. With this context there can then be a meaningful dialog about the changes in behavior being advocated for the future because they will understand the current and desired states.

From the beginning, the CISO must realize that metrics are created and collected to tell a story. They are used to explain how security services support the organization and its strategic objectives. We present the following to consider when creating metrics:

Metrics Principles

1. **Focus on the data.** Stay away from subjective assessments and focus on what can be measured and controlled. In other words, if we change behavior, the value of the metric should change.

2. **Know the purpose of the metric.** It should support a business goal. It must have context – "why are we collecting it, what story does it tell?"

3. **Measure what we need to know but report on what we want to change.** There will likely be a need to take dozens or possibly hundreds of measurements, but what we report on is what we want to focus attention on in order to change behavior. Everyone is overloaded, so focus on key signals and ignore noise.

4. **The data driving each metric should be easy to collect and analyze.** The process of collecting and aggregating the data and posting the metric should take no more than one third the length of its reporting frequency. If a report is weekly, it should take about two days to collect, process, and post.

5. **Know what "good" is.** We should know the target value we want to achieve.

6. **Whenever possible, state the metric in business terms.** "We have 100 servers with the 'Huckleberry' vulnerability" is meaningless to business leaders. "We have 100 servers with

the 'Huckleberry' vulnerability, 50 of which potentially expose our 'Goldenrod' product. A breach there would mean $50 million in hard costs and jeopardize $125 million in future revenue," tells the business why they care.

7. **We should know who acts based on the metric and what the action is.**

8. **Be consistent.** Report on the same metrics in the same way over an advertised and dependable frequency. Metrics should support trend data.

9. **Continually raise the bar.** When success is achieved as defined by any particular metric, de-prioritize or deprecate reporting on that measurement in favor of another behavior that needs to change, but spot check that metric to ensure that the progress is lasting and sustainable.

A Process Orientation

Now that we have the properties of good metrics, we can start looking at the specific metrics to include in reports. It is common for CISOs to measure control effectiveness and coverage along with the change in maturity and breadth of coverage over time.

An effective way to do this was outlined in Chapter 5 of the *CISO Desk Reference Guide* and consists of using the CMMI (Capability Maturity Model Integration) in conjunction with COBIT (Control Objectives for Information and Related Technology) which includes process steps and identifies checkpoints, called "key controls" or simply "controls," and selecting a standard (such as NIST 800-53 or CIS Critical Security Controls – formerly the SANS Top 20).

In addition to adopting and implementing controls based on the relevant technical standards, many organizations are subject to frequent audits of their security controls, and they often measure themselves according to compliance outcomes – successful audits, types and severity of findings, and change in severity and number of findings over time. In addition to these high-level metrics, audits for SOX, PCI, or ISO compliance can also be used to measure deviation from expected outcomes for the various and specific controls the organization maintains. Many organizations use these audits and assessments as their primary measurements and focus corrective action accordingly. We don't recommend that you use them as anything other than a trailing indicator (to measure improvement over time), as to do otherwise would be like using a smoke detector as a cooking aid. It is not likely to lead to an excellent (timely) result.

Business Objectives

Just as physical security measures don't prevent break-ins, digital security measures do not prevent breaches. They reduce the likelihood that any particular breach will result in a compromise of critical asset(s). They also help the organization prepare for a quicker recovery if critical assets are compromised, thus allowing the company to continue to meet its business objectives. We accomplish this reduction by providing layered protection and enough time for personnel to detect the initial breach and respond with appropriate countermeasures.

So how do we measure the ability to detect and respond? We can look at how quickly the security team and their partners close vulnerabilities, patch systems, address zero-days, identify and research the security events that the SIEM (security incident and event management) system recognizes, and how fast they deploy critical technologies (such as end-point protection or web application firewalls). Outside of measuring against specific operational goals, this gives us insight into how well our teams know our infrastructure and how easy or hard it is to address problems within that infrastructure.

A simple example would be that if a portion of the infrastructure is so fragile that it cannot be patched or rebooted, then that portion of the infrastructure is likely to be less resistant to attack and more difficult to recover. Likewise, if the staff has difficulty applying configuration changes due to lack of experience with specific component types, it is less likely they will be able to defend or rapidly recover those components successfully. On the other hand, while the ability to apply changes to a portion of the infrastructure might not indicate an above-normal ability to defend it from attacks, its stability would likely be an asset in reducing recovery time and allow the team to stay current with patches and upgrades.

Finally, it is also vital to track budgetary metrics such as percent of IT budget dedicated to cybersecurity or the number of personnel assigned to cybersecurity relative to the total number of employees in your organization, or other benchmarks that can assure leadership that resources are appropriately aligned or aligned similarly to peer organizations. While these types of metrics lack the granularity to pinpoint what specific changes an organization should make, they can provide a quick snapshot and surface essential questions such as:

- Why is it more (or less) expensive to deliver similar services?
- How do we achieve our goals with fewer personnel assigned?
- How do we compare to our peers?

Foundational Metrics

Security and risk management dashboards will be specific to the organization. It is best practice for executive management and the CISO to work together to develop a plan for the metrics to be presented.

Two examples:

Maturity Dashboards: present metrics that are used to represent the maturity of the organization's cybersecurity program. These dashboards can provide an overall assessment of the company's cybersecurity strategy in the context of the cybersecurity/risk management framework selected by the CISO. Other data points that might be monitored on a maturity dashboard are the results of previously identified issues. These results can be in various stages of remediation, and for governance purposes metrics can be used to monitor the progress of efforts to mitigate any identified problems.

Effectiveness Dashboards: provide insight to the CISO and senior management that allows them to ascertain the effectiveness of specific programs or projects.

- Cybersecurity threat assessment
- Cybersecurity threat detections
- Remediation metrics
- Recovery metrics

Here are some additional metrics that we think should be in every organization's metrics program. The metrics are categorized based on function and audience to facilitate collaboration. The CISO's role is to be the steward of the metrics process and ensure that the metrics decided upon will meet organizational requirements.

Administrative Metrics (Legal, Financial, HR)

<u>Legal</u>

- Percentage of material contracts that have been evaluated by the security function of the organization
- Percentage of all material contracts that require the evaluation of baseline security and privacy controls,

including specific requirements for breach notification and confidentiality language

Financial
- Percentage of IT budget allocated to cybersecurity. This percentage differs dramatically across sectors but stabilizes within sectors for organizations of all sizes. The average spend has been trending higher – expect a minimum of 8% and an average of 10%.

Human Resources (HR)
- Percentage of employees who have had a thorough background check, including investigation of previous criminal activity
- Percentage of job descriptions that highlight each employee's responsibility to protect the organization's assets
- Percentage of employees who have attended annual security awareness training and passed an assessment that demonstrates retention of core concepts
- Percentage of employees who have read, acknowledged and been tested on the organization's security policy as well as the acceptable use policy (AUP)

Vendor Management
- Percentage of material vendors who have been audited either directly by the organization's security function or via a third-party attestation (e.g., a SSAE 18 SOC 1 and/or SOC 2 audit)
- Percentage of material vendor relationships that are accurately and completely inventoried and documented by the organization

- Percentage of material vendors that participate in quarterly security reviews with the organization's security function

Operational Metrics (Security and IT Operations)

Asset (Software) Inventory
- Percentage of known assets accurately inventoried in an asset management system

Information (Data) Inventory
- Percentage of information assets accurately inventoried
- Percentage of information accurately classified
- Percentage of systems documented (e.g., via a data flow diagram)

System Upgrades and Patching
- Percentage of systems that are still supported by the manufacturer or a validated third party
- Percentage of systems patched within 30 days following notification of critical or security patches[11]
- Percentage of systems scanned for vulnerabilities on a monthly basis
- Percentage of systems configurations that reflect the hardening guidelines

Multi-Factor Authentication (MFA)
- Percentage of systems with IP, PII, ePHI, or other sensitive data that leverage MFA

---

[11] This metric will vary depending upon the maturity of your vulnerability management process and across systems depending on the amount of technical debt to overcome. It is critical that this metric receive special attention with an eye toward continuous improvement and a target of seven days.

Mean-Time-To-Incident Response and Remediation
- Mean time to incident response and remediation

Governance Metrics (Compliance)

Incident Response (IR) Plan
- Existence of a management-reviewed and approved IR Plan
- Date on which the IR plan was last tested (e.g., in a tabletop exercise)

Business Impact Assessment (BIA) Analysis
- Existence of a management-reviewed/approved BIA plan
- Date on which the BIA was last updated for changes to the business
- Number of high-risk business processes

Business Continuity / Disaster Recovery (BP/DR) Plans
- Existence of a management-reviewed/approved BC/DR plan
- Date on which the BC/DR plan was last tested
- Percentage of systems, processes, or applications that meet recovery-point objectives (RPO) and recovery time objectives (RTO)

The metrics above serve as guideposts for risk management and security operations. There are tens to hundreds of additional metrics that can be used, depending on the size and complexity of the organization. The metrics described above are designed to reduce high-risk blind spots within the organization and to ensure that, at a minimum, certain key planning documents (e.g., IR, BIA, BC/DR) exist, and specific core security functions (e.g., patch management, MFA, inventories, and vulnerability scanning) are in place.

Status on these metrics, even status that suggests real problems are present, should not be guarded within the security function. It is the

CISO's role, perhaps the primary purpose of the CISO's role, to ensure that his or her colleagues in IT, lines-of-business, executive management, and the board understand the fact pattern and consequences associated with these metrics. The CISO must ensure that the metrics are robust, and that clear communication tools are in place to inform the organization's stakeholders.

Strategic Measurements

The modern CISO needs to be a subject matter expert to help the CIO and CTO set technical direction for the enterprise, prepare for and respond to breaches, deal with the ever-expanding compliance and regulatory environment, and rapidly assess the impact of adopting new technologies or delivery platforms such as cloud computing, mobile, and BYOD. However, the modern CISO also needs to be able to build a highly effective human network. This human network needs to include the internal security team, cross-functional teams within the organization, and a sufficiently robust external network of peers, subject matter experts, counsel (both internal and external), law enforcement, vendors, and partners. The successful modern CISO will have regular contact with effective leaders internal and external to the organization that will help him or her understand the internal landscape, identify new threat vectors as they become relevant, and rapidly implement contingency plans as needed.

As we mentioned, the final measure of success is the strategic focus of the CISO. Successful CISOs must be force multipliers. Improving employee education, enhancing communications, insisting on collaboration, and making sure every employee plays their role in securing the organization's business processes will be the way the CISO ultimately makes the difference.

Key Insights and Recommended Next Steps

To effectively communicate the maturity of enterprise security efforts and ongoing risk mitigation initiatives to the security team, organizational peers, and senior leadership, the CISO will need to use metrics that provide relevant data, reports that provide actionable information, and dashboards that allow them to monitor information in real time. With this data, relevant parties can participate in a meaningful dialog about changes in behavior that are necessary to protect the enterprise and the CISO can lay out a future vision of a more risk tolerant organization. To be effective in communicating this picture to an organization's executive staff, business stakeholders, and third parties, the CISO needs to champion how cybersecurity supports the organization's business goals.

To accomplish this, collect metrics that contain relevant data and build dashboards that make the information actionable for the CISO, IT management, business stakeholders, and executive leadership. Ensure that reporting is tied to the organization's strategic objectives and only "... report on what you want to focus attention on in order to change behavior." In essence, ensure that the metrics being collected have a purpose. Use them to protect, to educate, and to drive collaboration and change.

Senior leadership and the board should work with the CISO to understand the meta messages that the metrics are providing. Ask and answer questions such as: what does the performance against the metrics tell us about the maturity, resilience, and adaptability of the organization? What are we learning? For example, do our patching metrics show brittleness or resilience of the infrastructure? How are our people doing and how do we adjust our awareness program based on the performance of the team against the metrics that track behaviors that affect security?

Section 2

The Cybersecurity Program

Introduction

In Chapter 7 we explore what we call **the human element**. We look at three elements of the greater team: identifying, attracting, and retaining the people the CISO will need to be successful, building what we refer to as the human network, and building a culture of security awareness and responsibility in the entire workforce.

Next, we discuss **situational awareness**. In Chapter 8 we tie threat intel, continuity planning, and security and program monitoring together into a cohesive approach that provides the executive team with a 360-degree view of the organization's security posture.

In Chapter 9 we tackle the most visible function for a typical CISO, **responding to cyber incidents**. As we mention in the executive summary for Chapter 9, incident response can no longer be a hot seat occupied only by the CISO. The executive management team, the CISO, and even the board of directors must share in the responsibility of preparing for and responding to cyber incidents.

Chapter 10 assembles all the elements we've discussed throughout the *CISO Desk Reference Guide Executive Primer* into **a cohesive program** and examines the tools the CISO will need to be successful as well as some specific ways the CISO's peers can provide critical support.

In Chapter 11 we provide a final, comprehensive view of the interrelationships between the CISO, the executive management team, and the board of directors. We explore the **unique roles of the CISO, the executive team, and the board** as well as the importance of proper tone at the top and appropriate expectations for and collaboration between each of these groups.

Chapter 7

The Human Element

The aim of a ship's captain is a successful voyage; a doctor's, health; a general's, victory. So the aim of our ideal statesman is the citizens' happy life--that is, a life secure in wealth, rich in resources, abundant in renown, and honorable in its moral character. That is the task which I wish him to accomplish--the greatest and best that any man can have.

~Marcus Tullius Cicero

Executive Summary

CISOs must recognize that they are always recruiting. Even if there is no unfilled headcount today, it will be necessary to create and maintain a pool of talented people. And while there is a minimum bar for the skills the security team will need to be successful, you can only hire for so many of those skills. The cost (in hard cost and opportunity loss) of competing for and hiring fully formed senior security engineers for all positions has already become prohibitive.

Short-term tactical advice for hiring is always useful but planning for the shift in when, from where and how work is done will be a vital medium-term objective. It will take a combination of human resource planning, government policy changes, new technology, and new approaches and capacity in our education systems to meet the need for talent. These changes will require us to work differently with partners and suppliers to achieve the outcomes we want. Organizations must accept that some security functions will be performed by third parties to allow the team to focus on areas that are strategic to the business.

The CISO must also focus on the broader team. The reality is that most successful breaches (including most incidents of ransomware) are initiated by relatively unsophisticated attacks. An effective cyber awareness program is critical to forming a robust defense against phishing and social engineering attacks.

The CISO should thoroughly understand their organization's objectives, strategy, and mission to implement an effective security awareness program. They should know what data and applications are important to their colleagues, understand the context of their functions in the broader context of the organization, and understand how their peers' line-of-business or executive functions facilitate the organization's overall strategy. This knowledge is invaluable. This background and context are the foundation of proper security awareness training directed at all members of the organization.

Talent and the Human Element

Let's put the first topic of this chapter, recruiting, in the broader context of talent management. As a discipline, talent management traditionally includes four pillars: recruitment, learning, performance, and compensation. This section focuses on recruitment and learning, which is done for an outcome (performance) at a price (compensation). Keep in mind that the purpose of talent management is to create a high-performing, sustainable organization that meets its strategic and operational goals and objectives. The goals we have for talent development are to allow the information security team to develop the skills and capabilities to continually adapt to changing business and threat environments. This will help the larger organization identify and manage the risks that threaten its information and operations technology and safeguard the organization's data (both generated and entrusted).

To successfully approach building and developing the team's capabilities, we need to consider the human element. We assert that each person's sense of purpose for their work is more indicative of their engagement and success than their skills. Our argument is that affinity is a more important predictor than efficiency.

That is not to say that skills aren't important. On the contrary, one has little chance of success without possessing the requisite skills for the job. We'd like to suggest that we think of the people we work with, who help us achieve our outcomes, as people, not just talent. We would like to hire the best people with the right skills and mindset, help them become even better at what they do, have them share a common set of goals, and have them engaged and happy to be part of our team for the long haul.

Hiring the right team includes a mix of seasoned individuals from outside the organization and individuals you nurture. You will use your network, internal and external, to help you identify and attract both.

Key Variables that Impact Recruiting Cyber Talent

Let's look at some of the variables that impact an organization's ability to recruit security talent.

Workforce Location - Recruiting managers and CISOs will need to balance in-office and remote personnel and design their work processes accordingly. This is a departure from long-standing norms, and it is imperative that CISOs quickly adapt to this reality. While this does remove geography as a barrier to recruitment, it also lowers the barrier for other organizations to recruit members of your team. In the post-COVID remote-first or hybrid work environment, organizations must open their recruiting approach to balance newfound workforce mobility. The good news is that the pool of candidates obviously expands dramatically when not tied to one given geography.

Budget - An organization's budget will have a critical role in attracting cybersecurity talent. Cybersecurity professionals are earning premiums over other IT roles. Organizations will need to anticipate paying more to attract cyber talent. However, how much more reflects the organization's specific context (e.g., risk tolerance, industry, profitability, use of third-party resources).

Reporting Relationships - To whom any professional reports and where their "manager" fits within the overall organization are essential considerations. Suppose a prospective employee is applying for a job reporting to a CISO buried within the organizational chart. This potential hire might infer that security is not a top priority for the company. If the CISO is not considered part of the organization's leadership team and widely respected, the CISO's and their manager's ability to attract talent will be challenged.

Risk Appetite - CISOs should align staffing levels and their team's competencies with the organization's overall risk appetite. An organization that is highly risk-tolerant is not likely to value investing in security personnel to the same level as an organization that is more risk-averse.

Corporate Culture and Industry - Do you know how the marketplace perceives your company? Does the organization need to refresh its image to be more attractive to prospective applicants? These questions are critical when recruiting cyber talent for your organization.

Skills and Experience Requested - Many hiring managers are guilty of drafting job descriptions that represent the ideal candidate, which are effectively job descriptions for candidates that just do not exist. Organizations should be realistic about the skills they need to fulfill the role and the number of years of experience required.

Industry Counts - Adapt your security recruiting efforts to your industry. Specific industries require unique competencies rarely found in candidates who have never worked in that field. If this is the case, ensure that your recruiting efforts target the social media sites, publications, and industry associations that the industry-knowledgeable candidates frequent.

Third-Party Service Delivery

Do not assume that a security professional on the security team must fill every security gap you have. Consider three questions about each potential position:

1. Is the best way to address this gap for the company to hire a person or contract with a trusted vendor?
2. Is this job best filled by a security professional with highly specialized skills?
3. With a limited security budget, is this a priority for security to hire instead of another department?

For question 1, the decision is whether it makes sense to outsource this function. Most executives at this point have learned to avoid the temptation to turn outsourcing into a purely financial decision. Finance is a factor, but so too, and often more important, are reducing management oversight burden, utilizing specialized skillsets that are difficult to acquire and difficult to maintain, and taking advantage of pools of talent and graduating levels of expertise that a single individual cannot bring to an organization. Question 2 highlights that there are certain skills, due to their specialization, that may not be required full-time by the organization (e.g., malware analysis and forensics) and may be candidates for third party services. The last question hits upon an important dynamic that many security functions may be addressed by other departments. Network security is a good example of this dynamic as firewall administration and network segmentation are frequently managed by IT teams versus the core security team.

Investing for the Long Term

There is widespread recognition that building the skills and competencies needed to improve the overall cybersecurity posture of our critical infrastructure requires national and coordinated attention. NIST's National Initiative for Cybersecurity Education (NICE) is focused directly on addressing this challenge. Special Publication 800-181 outlines the initiative.

NICE offers prescriptive detail regarding seven core security functions and 33 specialty areas of cybersecurity work. It defines 52 cybersecurity roles and provides the requisite knowledge, skills, abilities, and tasks for each role. NICE thereby helps organizations understand the types of skills and competencies required to comprehensively support a security program for the long term.

NICE provides insights and recommendations on necessary training within each core functional area to adequately address the function.

NICE, therefore, provides the foundation for your cybersecurity staffing program. With the NICE skills framework, educational organizations across the nation, including K-12 schools, trade schools, community colleges, technical institutes, and universities, can design programs to provide the critical training our workforce needs.

Motivating Cybersecurity Professionals

In the ESG-ISSA State of Cyber Security Professional Careers report,[12] researchers spoke with cybersecurity practitioners from all over the world. They asked them questions about their cybersecurity career, the health of the cybersecurity field as they viewed it, and why they worked as a CISO or senior cybersecurity professional. In this document, one of the more fascinating views into why people work in this field was the question of job satisfaction. The top five answers are:

1. Competitive compensation
2. Working with an organizational culture that supports cybersecurity
3. Business management's commitment to cybersecurity
4. Ability to work with highly skilled, talented people
5. Organization provides support and incentives to enable staff to receive training and improve skills

Security professionals want to serve and protect the organization. And they want to work with talented people and improve their skill sets, whether through classroom training, online training, or training exercises.

---

[12] The State of Cyber Security Professional Careers, by Jon Olstik, October 2016 (http://www.esg-global.com/hubfs/issa/ESG-ISSA-Research-Report-State-of-Cybersecurity-Professional-Careers-Oct-2016.pdf)

In a study conducted with Christine Porath, a professor at Georgetown University's McDonough School of Business, Tony Schwartz tells us that employees are vastly more satisfied and productive when we meet four of their core needs:

- physical, through opportunities to regularly renew and recharge at work;
- emotional, by feeling valued and appreciated for their contributions;
- mental, when they can focus in an absorbed way on their most important tasks and define when and where they get their work done;
- and spiritual, by doing more of what they do best and enjoy most and feeling connected to a higher purpose at work.

Given the difficulties of attracting cyber talent, investing the time and budget to ensure that retention efforts and employee satisfaction are paramount should be a priority for the CISO.

Essential New Facets of Diversity

Building diversity into our cybersecurity workforce allows us to tackle a broader range of problems and get to better, faster solutions more easily. CISOs must learn how to be relevant to the business and fluent in the language of business. A wonderful side benefit is how much the diversity of thought introduced by different models intended for different job disciplines helps problem-solving. People of varying job disciplines don't just solve problems differently; they bring different values and value different outcomes. We need to rethink recruiting to pull workers into cybersecurity from adjacent disciplines, not just adjacent fields. Building diversity into your workforce should include values derived from different work histories, job functions, and, of course, backgrounds.

Besides building diversity into the cybersecurity team, the organization should incorporate diverse job skills into the cyber awareness program. Advanced persistent threats (APTs) get much attention, but relatively unsophisticated attacks are the cause of most successful breaches. It's a matter of economics. Why would a hacker spend a lot of money and time on an APT, developing or purchasing custom exploits and/or zero days, when they can pay little or no money and get quick results using phishing or drive-by attacks? Using the whole workforce's skills, we can learn to effectively incorporate the personal value and social value of inherently secure processes into our daily routines. When our colleagues across the organization are trained to be aware of threats, they become an early warning system of potential attacks by reporting odd emails or text messages, unexpected messages on slack channels or other group chat tools, anomalous system behavior, and other concerns.

Awareness, Self-Defense, and a Shared Sense of Purpose

It has become a cliché: "Your employees are your first line of defense." Security professionals and standards writers agree, of course. NIST 800-53, ISO 27001, and PCI-DSS all devote portions of their standards to training and awareness. Also, attack postmortem analysis and employee response testing show that companies with security training programs decrease successful attacks by 20-40%.[13]

---

[13] Security Awareness Training Explosion, John P. Mello, Jr. (https://cybersecurityventures.com/security-awareness-training-report/)

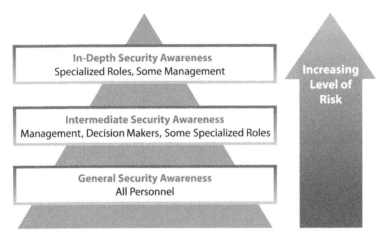

Figure 7.1 PCI Security Awareness Program Training Manual

One of the essential duties of a CISO is that of a change agent, especially when it comes to online cyber hygiene. From the diagram above, borrowed from the PCI Security Awareness Manual, we see that, in general, everyone should receive security training. The level and depth depend on the job role. The cyber education and awareness program should align with the corporate mission. Cyber hygiene needs to be prioritized, practiced, and taught by every executive, starting with the CEO. Every member of the C-suite must be signed up and evangelizing before you can have an effective cyber-awareness training program. Once this foundation is in place, you can start to address awareness, self-defense, and a sense of unity of purpose and shared outcomes.

The awareness program focuses on the reality of the threat, the depth of the ecosystem supporting the bad actors, and the cybercriminals' objectives. It should not focus on fear, uncertainty, and doubt (FUD). FUD seems on the surface to be a shortcut right to hyper-awareness of the challenges we face. But it often has the opposite effect as it makes the problem appear unsolvable. FUD creates a sense of hopelessness that leads to paralysis. It is usually sufficient to briefly explain the motives and frame the consequences in business outcomes (direct fraud, damage to the brand, IP theft, business disruption).

After establishing awareness, it's time to teach self-defense. Keep it simple: don't click, don't open, and don't reuse. We can try to explain more advanced concepts, but most successful attacks gain entry by enticing workers to click on links they should not click, open files they should not open, or by exploiting shared or reused passwords. We're not aiming for perfection at this stage, just trying to reduce the harmful behavior to the point that the automated tools have a fighting chance.

Finally, once the awareness and self-defense programs are rolled out and measured as effective, it's time to move on to coordinated behaviors and establishing a sense of unity of purpose and shared outcomes.

Historical Role Models

The general theme of civil defense is that civilians have a role in defending themselves, fending for themselves, and acting in a way that, at the very least, allows the public safety workforce the ability to focus more on the crisis at hand and less on the immediate safety of the civilian population. In the best of circumstances, civilians provide direct aid.

Another example is a coordinated and ongoing program to reduce accidents on the factory floor through awareness, training, and feedback loops that implement safety improvement suggestions from the workforce.

Each of these examples shares these key attributes:

- There is a coordinated effort required amongst both leadership and the population (or workforce)
- Diligence is demonstrated over an extended period

- An ecosystem that includes messaging, material, and roles and responsibilities is developed and rolled out
- The issue is of sufficient magnitude, and failure has personal, relatable consequences

How do you relate the consequences of poor cyber hygiene to your employees so that they take it personally, without scaring them into paralysis?

As with any communication plan designed to effect real change within your organization, the program needs to be thought out, there must be buy-in among the executive team, and the program needs to be rolled out with sufficient gravitas. If a training program already exists, assess it against the four attributes noted above and make sure it has the required impact.

Use the Language of Business

Those CISOs who excel at this translation from technical to business-focused risk frequently have their security programs well received by their colleagues, executive management, and ultimately and ideally, the board of directors. There are some relatively simple, pragmatic steps that CISOs can take to "train" their executive colleagues and the board on cybersecurity practices and why good security hygiene ultimately drives a resilient organization.

First and foremost, the CISO should know and thoroughly understand the organization's objectives, strategy, and mission. Equally important, the CISO should capture and inventory the unique strategies and objectives of colleagues and their respective departments within the organization. They should know how their counterparts are measured, know their motivations and goals, and know the context of their functions in the broader context of the overall organization. They should understand how their line-of-business or executive function facilitates the organization's overall strategy. This knowledge is invaluable. Background and context are the foundation of proper security awareness training directed at senior members of the organization. The CISO can then build an informal business impact analysis that links cyber risks to these various constituencies and their objectives.

For example, let's say that the sales team's focus is meeting sales quotas by developing a more personal knowledge of your organization's clients and prospects. As part of their effort, the sales organization needs to re-configure their customer relationship management (CRM) software to incorporate several new fields that help profile critical contacts within the client and prospective client organizations. Let's also assume that the CRM system's reconfiguration includes capturing highly sensitive detail on prospects and existing clients. It will now record details about hobbies, birthdays of their children and spouses, and their favorite wine. Exposure of this data in a breach or through an inadvertent employee error would create severe "reputational damage" to the organization.

Knowing how the Vice President of Sales' objectives translate into a high-risk strategy that could expose the organization to significant regulatory and reputational risk offers an opportunity to inject relevance into the cybersecurity awareness program. The risk treatment, including potential changes to security practices and the follow-on awareness campaign, is jointly developed by both teams and far more likely to address the risk without introducing process overkill.

Addressing Risk with Rigor

CISOs who have grown comfortable communicating with their business colleagues and senior executives can translate security and privacy risks into business and enterprise risk as second nature. They know the priorities of their colleagues and are well-versed in their organization's goals. They can readily position their security program as an enabler of these priorities under the best circumstances or as insurance should something go awry.

CISOs should establish periodic meetings with colleagues with a business-focused agenda. The meetings should seek to capture detail and confirm their understanding of the following:

- Core initiatives and the plans to achieve objectives
- Required changes to systems or data
- Key vendors and suppliers who are engaged in the initiative
- Other dependencies that could impact the initiative
- Timing and other constraints on the effort

The byproduct of these discussions is a valuable education for the CISO. It is also helpful as cyber training and awareness for the executive team. The CISO's colleagues and executive management benefit from the CISO's insights on cyber risk, especially related to digital technology. Ultimately, this collaboration creates an informed organization that is more resilient and better prepared to manage cyber risk.

There's another audience that is critical to this process, namely the board of directors. Boards have become increasingly concerned with cyber risk. High-profile breaches (notably the massive breach at Equifax), lawsuits directed at specific board members, and personal experiences with malware and spear phishing are all driving their desire to understand how prepared their organizations are to address a cyber-attack.

The work done by the CISO and their colleagues in looking at organizational priorities and initiatives, evaluating risk, and understanding the materiality of the organization's efforts serves as a solid foundation when the CISO is asked to present to the board on the preparedness of the organization. Instead of being blindsided by a new project that introduces significant risk, the CISO enters this presentation with the knowledge that they have been proactively engaged with business colleagues, evaluating cyber risk and making recommendations to bring that risk within acceptable business parameters.

Equally important, the discussions with other senior executives have translated technical risk into enterprise risk expressed in business terms. When presenting to the board, the CISO becomes a valued business leader, one versed in technical risk and with a strong working knowledge of the organization's risks and how to mitigate them. The CISO is effectively the board's trusted advisor on digital strategy.

Does Training Really Work?

To measure the effectiveness of your education program, look at the click-through rate on phishing (test this by targeting your workforce), look at the number of systems being infected with malware over a given period, validate password strength and change frequency in central identity stores, and engage your workforce in an ongoing dialog.

You'll know the education program is working when different departments are reaching out to the CISO because they have detected behaviors that are harbingers of imminent compromise, when departments report success and failure for cyber awareness on their own, and when members of the executive team are sharing best practices about what has worked for them and what hasn't. If the program continues to generate feedback about how confusing, unnecessary, and ineffective the cyber awareness training is, there is still work to do.

People want their work processes to be secure; they expect it; they demand it. But companies often make it so difficult for them to act securely, they become helpless. Helpless people do not feel empowered to act safely; they become resigned to being hacked, impersonated, and robbed.

As an example, no matter how hard we try, we are not going to get significantly better password management. Managing 100+ passwords will never be easy. Not having a password is easy. Writing rules about what kinds of passwords one can use and creating policies to enforce the rules only delights auditors and regulators. Therefore, part of any successful awareness program must be full transparency about the processes that need improvement and prominent coverage of the changes that are being made to the processes to make it easier to comply with security requirements. When the company moves to a password-less system, celebrate it. The team should know that processes are always getting better while showing plainly each person's role in making work processes cyber-safe.

Key Insights and Recommended Next Steps

It is essential to recognize that the CISO, and the entire information security team, are continually recruiting. Every opportunity to interact with the community is an opportunity to assess and impress the people who can help the organization succeed. Highly skilled individuals are motivated by a sense of purpose and opportunity to grow in addition to salary and traditional benefits. Given the depth and breadth of knowledge that a cybersecurity team must possess, it is almost impossible to acquire and maintain a staff that can do everything. Recognize that various third parties have virtual monopolies on specific expertise. The organization must balance delivering on its objectives and building for the future through strategic outsourcing.

The larger team must then mobilize to protect the organization from cyber-induced harm. It is critical to align the cyber awareness education program needs with the organization's goals for the program to be effective. While many cyber-related regulations mandate cyber awareness training, the CISO's job is to help the organization avoid the trap of administering the program as a mindless compliance activity. Each senior leader must recognize the value and be fully engaged in cyber awareness training to reduce threats to their business.

Best practices such as a review of lessons learned from security incidents can also play a vital role in the cyber awareness program (even when these are pulled from the headlines if your organization is fortunate enough to lack first-hand incidents to review). The cyber awareness education program is critical to achieving cyber resilience, so CISOs should collect metrics that both directly measure the cyber awareness program (such as familiarity with messaging) and indirectly measure its effectiveness (such as click-through rates on phishing campaigns). Never underestimate the human element and its value for your security program.

Chapter 8

Situational Awareness

...do not spare any reasonable expense to come at early and true information; always recollecting, and bearing in mind, that vague and uncertain accounts of things [are]... more disturbing and dangerous than receiving none at all.

~George Washington

Executive Summary

We grouped these three process elements – threat intelligence, continuity planning and cyber-resilience, and monitoring – together because, when taken as a whole, they provide the organization with situational awareness about their security posture.

There is a tendency to believe that once something like threat intelligence is packaged commercially, that "buying" your threat intelligence is the most comprehensive and practical approach. Let the experts collect the data from their millions of sensors and their honeypots and other forms of deception technology, and let their analysts review that intelligence and monitor the dark web for you and tell you where you should focus your attention. It's true that very few companies have the means to run a comprehensive threat intelligence program on their own, and even those that do still consume commercial feeds to support their efforts. But there is a critical aspect to threat intelligence that is specific to each organization.

Continuity planning was once the exclusive province of the CIO. But the emerging role of the CISO, beyond expertise in cyber risk, policy, and data protection, is the continuity of business operations. To be successful, CISOs need to bring risk management front and center and make it a cornerstone in building their security programs. We cannot protect every system equally. Not all business processes, applications, and infrastructure are created equal. This inequality may seem obvious, but our security programs frequently don't reflect this reality. Too many security programs attempt to apply the same level of security to all systems, infrastructure, and employees. The result is watered down security. Critical systems are under-resourced and under-secured while non-critical systems are over-protected. The root cause of this disconnect is a lack of alignment with organizational priorities.

Networks are noisy. From heartbeats to probing, from legitimate database extracts to covert data exfiltration, from sensor telemetry to malware infusions, there is an enormous amount of traffic on your network. Without a strategic and diligent approach, it is difficult to know how much of this traffic is appropriate and legitimate. Long gone are the days when network traffic volume alone was the biggest hint that an organization was under attack. When we think of monitoring, many of us immediately think of our networks and the packets that traverse them. It's our view that this monitoring, while crucial to our security programs, is only a small part of the overall effort. CISOs must take a more comprehensive and expansive view of monitoring to ensure that they adequately align their security program with the objectives of their organization.

Threat Intelligence

Introduction

Threat intelligence, like situational awareness, is the discipline of becoming conscious of the environment in which you are operating with the intent of decreasing the potential impact of harms that are presented to you or your community. CISOs need to use a combination of data about the relevant threat actors and the vulnerabilities of the organization's high-value assets along with their judgment about the combinations that pose the greatest risk to the organization. This will allow them to inform the people on their team about the current threats that they should focus on, how to recognize them, how to prepare for them, and how to defend against them. This also refers to understanding specific vulnerabilities and the techniques that might be used to exploit those weaknesses in a way that your people and your defensive systems can immediately use to prevent or mitigate specific threats. Threat intelligence can also refer to specifics about the adversaries (who is posing a threat) and the victims (who is the target). Good threat intelligence should be actionable; you need to know what the adversaries want to do, to which companies, applications, and systems, and you need to know if and how that applies to your organization.

Threat Intelligence Is More Than a Service

It is also easy to get overwhelmed by the sheer volume of threat intel. But there is another aspect to threat intelligence that involves work that CISOs do on behalf of their organization. The need to create a 360-degree view of the environment in which the organization operates creates an excellent opportunity for the CISO to work with their human network, especially their external network of peers, subject matter experts, law enforcement, vendors, and partners.

If your organization has a relationship with local law enforcement through its physical security organization, the CISO should partner with that group and leverage that connection. Minimally, this involves local law enforcement, such as city police departments, county sheriff's departments, and state troopers across the United States. Absent other federal relationships, the CISO would often connect with the FBI (through regional associations such as InfraGard) and the Department of Homeland Security (DHS).

The emphasis here is on the human network, which we have identified as your network of peers, subject matter experts, law enforcement, vendors, and partners. CISOs should meet regularly with these colleagues and build trust relationships with the people with whom they can effectively partner. The informal human network serves as an invaluable source of threat intelligence, from pooled and shared feeds to side-channel discussion to a short list of who to call and who might warn of impending threat. Which organizations do we share our cyber threat knowledge with, and what are we learning from them? What is our working (information sharing) relationship with the most high-profile firms who have had breaches? Do we have information coming to us from them? What have we learned? When we hear of a breach in another organization, what do we do? When does that process start, and what is the routine reporting in the organization? What are the criteria that determine who to notify and when to notify the board of directors?

As we look at the data for intrusions, penetrations, or attempts to gain unauthorized access, what has been the primary category of threat actors who seem to have made these efforts? How has that information influenced our defensive efforts? This question challenges us to do more with the output of our scanning and testing programs than just patching the vulnerabilities we discover. There are various kinds of indicators of compromise, such as the presence of a piece of malware known for specific types of attacks, customized spear-phishing emails, inappropriate authentication attempts against assets, and evidence of targeted unauthorized scans against our network. When we detect these indicators, we should develop a working theory of the methods used to attack our assets, and by whom, so that we can improve our countermeasures against the immediate threat and future threats as well. We should also share as much of this information as we safely can with our partners in law enforcement, our vendors, our colleagues, and our peers.

Contextualized Threat Intelligence

Threat intelligence without context is just a laundry list of threats that create fear, uncertainty, and doubt in some scenarios and the "boy who cried wolf" syndrome in others. To build a good threat intelligence program, CISOs need to understand what they are protecting. Specifically, they need to know their industry, their employees and key stakeholders, their organization's processes, the applications that support these processes, and the underlying infrastructure (operating systems, hardware, and networks). CISOs need to bring the context to their program.

Know your industry: Certain industries have intrinsically higher risk than others. The defense industry's threat landscape differs dramatically from that of the agricultural sector. Analyze the dynamics of your industry. Do you face stiff international competition? Is the industry consolidating? Do you collect and retain sensitive information as part of your industry's business model?

Know the profile of your business: While there are common threads across industries and sectors, internal dynamics within your organization are equally important and provide a crucial contextual foundation for your threat intelligence program. Have a clear understanding of your organization's board of directors and executive management. Do they have unusually high profiles in your industry? Are they targets? Understand how your organization derives its income. Which markets does it sell to? What is a typical client profile?

Know the critical business processes or functions of your organization: Understand the basic process flow and key participants in each critical business process. Validate whether the process would impact the confidentiality, integrity, or privacy of the organization's information, should availability be interrupted. With operational technology more frequently connected to traditional networks, you should determine whether an issue with an operational process or function (e.g., manufacturing) would impact the safety of employees or clients and whether there's the potential to create physical damage to the organization's assets.

Know which applications support specific processes: Document and inventory those applications that directly support essential organizational functions and processes and who has administrator access to these applications. Your inventory of applications should include relevant details including the application's manufacturer, its version, and other pertinent information that will provide context related to the application. Don't overlook SaaS and hosted applications. Your security tools and applications should also be vetted and inventoried. Inventory software developed in-house and capture detail related to its development, including who was on the development team. Find out whether they are still part of the organization. If they've left, who has assumed responsibility for the application's ongoing care? Where is the source code maintained (e.g., on-premises or in a hosted repository)? Who has access to this source code? As we have seen with the SolarWinds and Kaseya exploits, enterprise software has become a key adversarial target. Determine how your organization evaluates patches from software suppliers and other assurances (e.g., hashes and certificates related to software code).

Know your infrastructure: For every critical application you have identified, you should also have a good understanding of the operating system it runs on, which server or virtual machine the OS is running on, and its storage, network, and backup dependencies. Know the hardware manufacturers, the versions of the firmware, and the status of all OS and firmware updates. This level of detail can make the difference between a well-managed response to a known issue versus a panicked "what's our exposure to 'x' or 'y' issue?"

Know your vendors and suppliers: One thing the well-publicized Target breach[14] taught us is that our vendors can have a material impact on our security operations. In case we forgot, the SolarWinds incident[15] certainly provided a painful reminder. Create an inventory of your vendors, including the major software applications your firm uses. Collaborate with your procurement team to make sure you include basic security expectations in vendor and service provider contracts. Make sure that you can adequately map vendors and suppliers to specific business processes and functions. Know the details related to your SaaS providers.

Sources of Intel

To use threat intelligence effectively, CISOs need to make some decisions about which sources they wish to use.

Internal threat intelligence is information that is within the organization. It is information that an organization's security and operations teams have from previous experiences with vulnerabilities,

---

[14] Target targeted: Five years on from a breach that shook the cybersecurity industry, Lisa Myers, Dec 2018
(https://www.welivesecurity.com/2018/12/18/target-targeted-five-years-breach-shook-cybersecurity/)
[15] A 'Worst Nightmare' Cyberattack: The Untold Story of The SolarWinds Hack, Dina Temple-Raston, April 2021
(https://www.npr.org/2021/04/16/985439655/a-worst-nightmare-cyberattack-the-untold-story-of-the-solarwinds-hack)

malware incidents, and data breaches. This information, if properly documented, can provide meaningful insights into earlier compromises of the enterprise's networks. It can also highlight recurring methodologies that worked against your security program.

External threat intelligence is threat intelligence that is available from multiple sources outside the organization. These external sources can be subscriptions or "feeds." These feeds can be consumed directly by the organization's security appliance (such as a SIEM) for a monthly fee. Alternatively, these feeds can be reports that you receive via email or from a threat portal where you can download the data that apply to your organization. Another type of external threat intelligence feed could be specific to your organization's industry.

CISOs need to select data feeds that are relevant to the organization, the industry and locations in which it operates, and the technologies and applications deployed in its business portfolio. CISOs should understand how the threat information relates to the organization so that it provides maximum risk mitigation.

Good Follow-Up Is Essential

Good threat intelligence should be actionable. When we learn of threats, we should have a process by which we determine if it applies to our organization, how to assess the nature of the threat, and the type of assets at risk. Do we have similar assets? What is the method of attack? Are we susceptible to that attack? What breaches have occurred, and could the same attack scenario work against us?

Sometimes that is a simple question to answer – we might know that we do not have the same kinds of assets – and sometimes that is a very complicated question to answer – we might need to perform a vulnerability scan or stage a penetration test or another form of security review to find out. Once we know that an attack could work, and we determine that the assets at risk are worth taking extra measures to protect, we need to validate that a breach has not occurred, and then patch, upgrade, disable, backup, and take whatever other actions we deem appropriate to protect against that attack scenario.

Monitoring the national news media is another valuable source of threat intelligence, but with an interesting caveat. Effective threat intelligence programs should make you aware of threats that are specific to your industry before you read about them in the national news. Public opinion can create a sense of crisis very quickly, and that sense of crisis can either amplify the threat to your organization or generate concern within your organization, from management, the workforce, or the board of directors. This fear can, in turn, create an urgency to act. Knowing that threats specific to your industry are active before the national news broadcast can give CISOs a critical head start to understand the danger, devise an action plan, and prepare to execute that plan without an aura of crisis.

Continuity and Cyber-Resilience

Introduction

Resiliency is at the heart of cybersecurity. No organization is immune from being attacked. In fact, our organizations are subject to ongoing and in many cases highly persistent attacks. The CISO's job is to ensure that their organization remains resilient when confronted with risks, be they cyber or natural disasters. In the context of an organization's business continuity plan, there are a few fundamental concepts that are especially important. We first mentioned the Business Impact Analysis (BIA) in Chapter 6 as the possible subject of metrics: do you have one, how recent is it, what are the high-impact business processes? As input for continuity planning, the BIA becomes critical. At a minimum, you'll need to know operational impacts (the impact on customers, the impact on back-office functionality), financial impacts (lost revenue, expense impact), and technological dependencies (systems, networks, sequencing, etc.) of each business process you identify.

Defining, Documenting, and Mitigating Risk

As we mentioned in the executive summary, the consequences of blanket, cover-all approaches to security are challenging. Unless the organization benefits from an ever-expanding budget and nearly unlimited resources, the reality of a protect-everything-equally security program is watered down security. Critical systems are under-resourced and under-secured while we effectively overprotect non-critical systems. The root cause of this disconnect is a lack of alignment with organizational priorities.

To facilitate a successful risk discussion, the CISO should capture and understand the organization's overall risk appetite concerning the impacts on the confidentiality, integrity, availability, privacy, and even the safety of material business processes. These impacts need to be formally aligned with enterprise risk management and specific risk considerations for the organization related to financial, reputational, operational, and other higher-level risk considerations.

When done correctly, a risk-focused discussion translates detailed technical risk into business terms which senior executives and the board can more readily consume and act upon. Executive management and the board are concerned about the impacts of an adversary on the organization, its reputation, and its finances, even if they are not well-versed on their tactics, techniques, and procedures (TTPs).

CISOs should continually ask themselves: "What is it that I don't know that I should know about this business process or initiative that could impact the confidentiality, integrity, availability, privacy, and safety of the process?" This open-ended question keeps the focus on considerations that could materially impact the organization. The business impact analysis can facilitate this line of questioning. Which dependencies and risk factors – notably from a cyber perspective – could negatively influence those processes that are most critical to the organization?

Keeping Executive Management and the Board of Directors Adequately Informed

CISOs should ensure that they are well-versed in the organization's core strategy and play an integral role in overseeing and informing risk management activities. Part of the CISO's role is to ensure that cyber risks that could impact the strategy or mission of the organization are understood, documented, and treated in a manner consistent with the entity's risk tolerance. If the CISO is not sure what the organization's risk tolerance is, they need to ask questions until it's clear. It is equally important to validate this understanding with other stakeholders in the organization. CISOs should also ask these questions periodically because risk tolerances can change.

Given the near-constant news about the compromises of companies and government agencies, executive management and the board will want to know just how secure the organization is. There should be ongoing discussions between CISOs and executive management and the board about the risk profile of the organization. CISOs will have a more receptive audience for their recommendations if they review and assess threats and risks to the organization's core functions and strategy as opposed to risks to the infrastructure. CISOs should always convey the risks to the organization in business terms that highlight the potential impact on reputation, financial exposure, regulatory compliance, contractual obligations, and operational considerations.

Business Continuity Planning Is a Strategic Process

The goal of business continuity is to continue business operations through uncertain times until re-establishing a level of normalcy. It is not always necessary to activate the Business Continuity Plan (BCP) during an incident. However, disaster recovery procedures (DRP) do get activated during a business-impacting incident. The focus of the DRP is on re-establishing corporate IT networks and cybersecurity controls to return operations, assets, and services to normal. The first stage of creating the DRP is to list critical assets, their threats, and the organization's prevention, response, and recovery strategies. Look to the organization's BIA for additional important context.

Disaster Recovery Critical Assets & Recovery Procedures (High Level)

Critical Asset	RTO/RPO	Threat	Prevention Strategy	Response Strategy	Recovery Strategy
ERP System	4 Hours / 2 Hours	Server Failure	• Secured Server Room • Secondary Server • UPS	• Switch to backup server • Validate UPS operational	• Repair primary server • Transition back to primary connection or server
Web Portal	2 Hours / 1 Hour	Loss of online sales portal	• Failure Alerts • Redundant Internet Circuits • Redundant Web Server	• Switch to backup internet connection or web server • Verify database and payment connections	• Repair internet connection or web server • Transition back to primary connection or server

Figure 8.1 High-Level Procedure View[16]

These processes incorporate additional inherent risks by potentially superseding, at least temporarily, cybersecurity controls. Activating emergency standby systems or granting third-party service providers emergency access to systems and data sometimes circumvents standard controls for system configuration, identity and access management, storage management, and backups. It's this pervasive operational risk that provides the call for the CISO's involvement in the development of their organization's BCP program.

---

[16] This table is reproduced from Chapter 14 of the *CISO Desk Reference Guide, Volume 2*, CISO DRG Publishing – Bonney, Hayslip & Stamper

Consider these dependencies:

People – Which staff and contractors are required for the system? If there is a shortage of a specific skill set or system knowledge, consider training staff and whether a third party or contractor may be required.

Facilities – Can the identified assets be ported into the cloud, or do they need to be in a datacenter? Another issue to consider is where will the emergency staff who are part of the BCP and DRP process operate from?

Supporting Technology – Which supporting technologies will be required for critical assets to work? This includes room for the emergency equipment, HVAC, sufficient primary and secondary power, availability of rollover, and so forth.

Data – Are there issues with the data (e.g., where the data is located, how it is backed up, and on what media)? Also identify who requires access to the data and for what purposes. Do the same people have data requirements during an emergency as during normal operations?

Supply Chain – Will there be a requirement for alternative suppliers for services? Identify supplier requirements and if new contracts are required, put them in place to ensure that the BCP activation process is smooth and efficient with no interruption to third-party services.

After documenting and reviewing the elements listed above, stakeholders must create the second stage of the DRP. Take the strategy for each identified critical asset and develop step-by-step procedures to recover the asset during a business continuity event. Ensure this documentation is readily available for stakeholders should a significant issue occur. Data from the tables developed during the asset strategy sessions will be required to create the disaster recovery procedures.

The BCP and DRP programs that reach throughout the business are like the CISO's enterprise security program. All three programs can profoundly influence operations and strategic business decisions. Having a mature BCP and DRP program within the company dramatically benefits the CISO, their security team, and their ability to address risk during critical cyber incidents.

Leveraging the BCP and DRP for Cyber Resilience

The BCP is an organization-wide program that encompasses people and processes and their responses to an emergent event. The DRP also contains data on people and processes, but it includes a third critical element. This third element is technology, and the DRP focuses on the strategic processes required to return technology, IT infrastructure, and associated services to operational order. These two programs are intertwined, and many of their workflows feed one another. From a high-level view, the BCP anticipates business disruptions and plans for the rapid restoration of business operations through the DRP process. Both programs contain extensive information that can be used by the CISO to enhance security operations.

It is also critical to identify and communicate the most critical systems and the sequence of recovery. Depending on the interdependencies, you may need to re-establish enabling processes before recovery can be attempted or even started. This requires significant coordination between senior staff during a major outage. This implies using a scale for the criticality of business processes to allow the allocation of appropriate resources for recovery – Low (outage has little impact), Moderate (moderate impact on the organization), High (disruption would cause the most impact). The BIA will help define this scale as noted in recovery point and recovery time objectives.

With the organization's processes so labeled, the CISO can plan their backup strategy. The organization determines the criteria for what constitutes low, moderate, and high impact. Once the CISO has prepared a preliminary model, they should cost it out and make sure the organization can afford what they've scoped. Conversely, the CISO should understand the impact of what they classify as moderate and low and determine if the business can live with potential system degradation or service unavailability. They should also note where their organization is on its cloud adoption journey. Cloud services can frequently complement and support BCP and DRP efforts.

Monitoring Your Environment

Introduction

The goal for most hackers is to remain invisible in their targeted environment for as long as possible (i.e., "low and slow"). The reasons vary, but the key ones are to afford the hackers the time to sufficiently map the infrastructure and identify the high-value assets to target for exfiltration or destruction and to establish means for persistence in the environment. There are exceptions such as ransomware, false flag operations, and misdirection, but in general, hackers aren't likely to rattle around in your network with tons of pop-up messages and chat requests. Unfortunately, security tools don't come with a "Spot the Hacker" button either.

Just how good is the security program? Every CISO needs to ask this question continuously. So too should their colleagues in executive management as well as the board of directors. How the CISO frames this question is equally important. In basic terms, is the security program reducing risk to a business-acceptable level? Cyber risk is a component of enterprise risk management (ERM), albeit a type of risk that is often more nuanced and complex to qualify and quantify than other, more traditional, risk management disciplines such as financial and operational risk. Monitoring the security program is key to determining if the organization's risk profile and appetite are consistent with the organization's overall strategic goals and objectives.

We Can No Longer Rely on the Castle and Moat Defense

We have witnessed the disappearance of the traditional network perimeter due to trends such as permitting personal devices at work and especially remote-first initiatives popularized as a response to the COVID-19 pandemic.[17] We now have semi-permeable gateways where our firewalls and network or enterprise boundaries used to be. But we're dealing with persistent cybercriminals who want to hang out in our networks indefinitely if we let them. They will use the easiest method possible to gain access but will stop at nothing to achieve their objectives, notably those threat actors who have nation-state backing. Given the ease of gaining access and the desire for persistence, we must have a comprehensive technical monitoring program, one that recognizes that traditional perimeters rarely exist.

The monitoring program should start with routine sweeps of file systems for malware, reviews of access log files, responses to help desk tickets, and a root cause analysis for application errors and network failures. Don't overlook other logs and events, including failed authentication attempts, data transfer logs, and error logs. There should be a current inventory of applications, including whether the application is off the shelf or custom built, on a current or deprecated technology stack, with current licenses and maintenance contracts.

---

[17] According to the IBM 2021 Cost of a Data Breach report, the average cost of a data breach where remote work is a factor is 24.2% higher than where remote work was not a factor.

What Should You Be Looking For?

What other types of technical monitoring should the security team do? Depending on the industry and the size of the target painted on the data you are protecting, consider the following:

- Monitor the network for vulnerabilities.

- Monitor the network for unauthorized scanning and realize this probing will be patient and stealthy.

- Monitor the dark web for activity about the organization. If this is not something you can staff directly, consider threat intelligence services that include monitoring of a range of data points, including the dark web.

- Conduct penetration testing on the network.

- Validate least privilege and network segmentation principles for your network and the departments and functions that network segmentation supports.

- Review the configuration drift from approved secure baselines for both physical and virtual assets.

- Review the third-party applications and accounts (approved and unapproved) deployed on or accessed from your network. Pay special attention to service accounts.

- Continuously monitor all remote network connections to your network.

- Review the events generated by system accounts.

Monitoring the Non-Technical Security Posture

While technical monitoring is a critical activity, it is only a small part of the overall effort. CISOs must take a more comprehensive and expansive view of monitoring to ensure that they adequately align their security program with the objectives of their organization.

The premise is that there is essential, not necessarily technical, risk context that can influence the success of the security program. The goal of security program governance monitoring is to go from a reactive security posture to a proactive, informed, and engaged security posture. Here are some of the critical elements of your security program for governance monitoring:

- **Legal Obligations**: Ensure that the organization's security practices are consistent with contractual and regulatory obligations. The proactive CISO will review these obligations in advance of the organization entering into any material agreement and establish a collaborative environment with the organization's counsel, be it internal or external.

- **Regulatory Obligations**: Ensure that the organization's security practices are consistent with state, federal, and international laws such as the European Union's General Data Protection Regulation (GDPR). Specifically, the CISO should be aware of and validate whether the security program is meeting the intent of the law.

- **Program Budget**: Understand the financial costs of delivering proper security for the organization, including the status of the security infrastructure. Are any systems close to being declared end-of-life? Are there maintenance and subscription fees (notably for threat intelligence services) that are coming due? Are there risks that are not adequately treated given funding?

- **Procurement and Line-of-Business Initiatives**: Seek out details related to the procurement of third-party services and initiatives from colleagues across different lines of business within the organization. Evaluate which services the organization uses that the security team or IT do not control.

Collectively, this context helps to inform the security program and allows management to gauge whether current capabilities are consistent with the organization's objectives for business resilience.

Key Insights and Recommended Next Steps

We grouped these three process elements – threat intelligence, continuity and cyber-resilience, and monitoring – together because, when taken as a whole, they provide the organization with situational awareness about their security posture. For threat intel, it's not just about what the bad guys are saying on the dark web and the latest strain of ransomware. While important, it is equally important to put this in the context of how it applies to your organization and its unique operating context. What makes your organization more (or less) vulnerable? What can you do about it?

Armed with that knowledge, it is critical to act. Early in the internet era, it was not uncommon for executives to downplay input from security professionals, believing the risk was low. Fortunately, those days have passed. Unfortunately, legal and regulatory jeopardy along with cybercriminal activity and climate-driven business interruption have increased exponentially and frankly left us no choice but to act prudently and prepare the organization for the inevitable incident. This preparation has proved invaluable in responding to the COVID-19 pandemic and while there is still much to do, companies are becoming more resilient to cyberattack every day.

There are two sides to the preparedness coin. One side is being prepared with incident response, business continuity and disaster recovery plans. The other side is being aware of the current state and knowing when and how to act. Taken together, you know what to look for, how to act when you need to, and when to take the actions you've prepared to take. To that end, the CISO should work with the senior leadership team to ensure that the incident response plan, business continuity plan, and disaster recovery plan adequately address cyber incident preparedness and that the teams are fully prepared. Additionally, the board should require periodic updates on the organization's monitoring activities, including the threat intelligence program, to maintain its high-level situational awareness.

Chapter 9

Incident Management

In all matters, before beginning, a diligent preparation should be made.
~Marcus Tullius Cicero

Executive Summary

Incident response is the most visible function for a CISO and how the CISO oversees the incident response program is critical for the role. For good or for ill, it is the primary way CISOs are judged. Beyond the immediate impact of demonstrating the organization's resilience to customers, management, and employees, how an organization deals with incident response says a lot about its culture. We have entered the era of the celebrity breach. Often nation-state sponsored, sometimes impacting millions of customers, and always coming with tiring lists of remediation steps that are at the same time both complex and monotonous in their sameness. We have long since worn out the cliché of "not if but when" as we describe the inevitability of a data breach happening to any given company. Making the front page of the *New York Times* because of a cataclysmic data breach was once an existential threat. Now, there is a certain resignation to the fact that data breaches are a part of life. Incident response can no longer be a hot seat occupied only by the CISO, as responding to an incident must be a team effort.

Incidents can escalate quickly (and publicly) so the organization should be prepared to communicate just as quickly to regain the narrative. Each member of the senior leadership team should understand their role in preparation activities, communication plans, escalation paths, and decision making. Cross training is also essential. Team members in all disciplines, including senior leaders, get sick and take vacations and are therefore unexpectedly unavailable.

Management should ensure that communications templates are prepared in advance. These communications templates should identify for whom the message is intended, what to communicate, who will publish, and under whose authority. When customers are demanding answers and public forums are being used to discuss or amplify the issue, your ability to respond rapidly is critical for de-escalating the issue.

Introduction

Cybercriminals are successfully targeting and compromising businesses of every size across all industry sectors. This ongoing digital onslaught demonstrates the need for organizations to be prepared to respond to the inevitable data breach. Incident response is the most visible function for a CISO and is the primary way CISOs are judged. How well this role is supported demonstrates whether the organization recognizes the challenges and opportunities of doing business in the twenty-first century.

Quickly recognizing and responding to incidents can be the difference between a minor disruption and a major breach. Communicating effectively during an incident is also critical to maintaining the confidence of the organization's many stakeholders, and preparation is the key to success. Organizations can demonstrate value in their incident response program by first understanding that the business must be the focus. Once the organization realizes that incident response is about staying in business, not playing spy-catcher or whack-a-hacker, investing in incident response becomes investing in the organization, its customers, and its people.

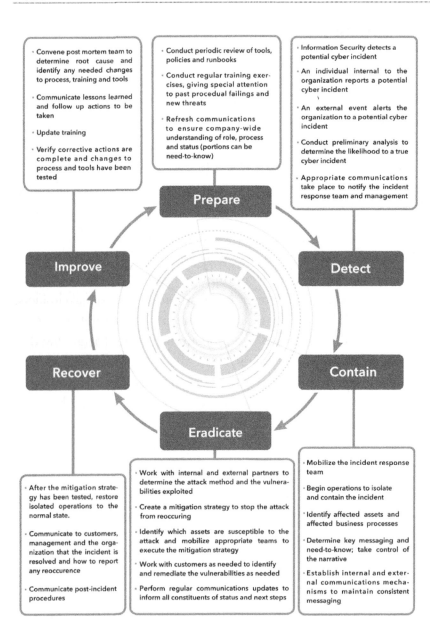

Figure 9.1 Incident Response Virtuous Cycle[18]

---

[18] This table is reproduced from Chapter 15 of the *CISO Desk Reference Guide, Volume 2*, CISO DRG Publishing – Bonney, Hayslip & Stamper

Incident Management

Phases of Incident Management

Figure 9.1 depicts the six phases of incident management as a familiar "virtuous cycle." In the *CISO Desk Reference Guide, Volume 2*, we dedicated chapters 15, 16, and 17 to incident response, incident recovery, and the aftermath. Incident response covers the prepare, detect, contain, and eradicate phases. Incident recovery maps to the recovery phase and includes resuming operations. It is during the aftermath of an incident that forensic and post-mortem activities occur, which is captured in the improve phase. You'll notice that all six phases have communication activities. From preparing, to messaging in the heat of the battle, to sharing lessons learned, timely, direct and accurate communication is vital.

Preparation Is Key

To be able to respond to incidents or potential incidents as they occur, the organization must identify and train one or more individuals and empower them to take appropriate action. This training includes how to triage potential incidents to determine the likelihood and potential severity and who to call (management, vendors and partners, law enforcement) to escalate incidents that they are not able to resolve on their own. They should know the key data elements to capture when cataloging or escalating an event as this information will be vital at later stages of incident response.

Beyond these "first responders," the entire organization should be trained to recognize and report issues that may constitute a cyber incident. This training is analogous to the security mantra: "If you see something, say something." Many people are afraid or at least hesitant to raise an issue because of a perceived risk that what they surface might turn out to be benign. They might wish not to distract precious resources from more critical tasks, or they might be embarrassed to raise a false alarm. Everyone should know the basics so they have confidence in what they report, but there should be an easy way to raise the alarm without having to perform a technical assessment. Empower your employees to be part of the solution.

The organization should conduct regular tabletop exercises with representatives from every function that simulates real life scenarios. Best practice is that representatives of the entire organization are rotated through training to avoid the trap of having departments "assign" the training to junior people who aren't truly representative of their groups.

Communications templates should identify for whom the message is intended, what to communicate, who will publish, and under whose authority. When the user community is demanding answers via social media or some other public forum is being used to discuss or amplify the issue, your ability to respond rapidly can de-escalate the issue and allow your organization to regain the narrative.

Another vital step in preparing to respond to cybersecurity incidents is to set aside emergency funds and establish an emergency procurement process. The difference between incident and catastrophe is containment and, in some circumstances, the CISO may have to engage specialized quick-reaction teams that would need to be on the job in hours. Using the normal procurement channels including RFPs and purchase approvals is untenable in a fast-moving emergency.

Incident Management Requires Incident Governance

What follows are the key activities that will help the organization provide good governance for its incident response program and the incident response plan and runbooks for common scenarios (e.g., compromised credentials, ransomware, phishing, lost or stolen devices, malware), including key roles for executive leadership and the board of directors, and the corresponding communication objectives within those activities.

Balancing resource needs across competing objectives is a critical function of the board and a key requirement for effective governance. The organization must be adequately staffed, equipped, and trained to deal with cyber incidents. The board should take a lead role in ensuring that the organization is prepared to rapidly recover in the event of a disruption caused by cyber incidents and validate the preparations made to ensure business continuity. At the least, this would include allocating time on the board agenda to review plans and ask probing questions. For particularly complex organizations it may make sense to subject the plans to audit review.

Frontline personnel need to know who to call, and under which circumstances to make that call. The escalation path is critical to being able to bring the situation under control rapidly. Senior management must ensure that the escalation path includes people at the correct level, with the proper authorizations, and with the proper skillset to make critical decisions. The early choices for containment and communications are the most important. At a crucial point, the skillset needed to make necessary containment decisions will give way to the skillset required to decide on appropriate recovery options, such as restoring in place or switching to alternate resources, such as a warm data center or temporary facility or using complementary systems in public clouds.

Public officials are also part of the escalation path. While there are regulatory conditions for breach notification that come with the threat of sanction for not meeting the requirements, there is usually enough time between the onset and conclusion of an incident and the close of the notification period. The more immediate need is to involve law enforcement at the right point if there is reasonable suspicion that a crime is being or has been committed and to involve regulators as needed depending on the nature of the incident and the industry. The best way to know the right point for escalation to law enforcement or notification of regulators is to involve them in the preparation activities. This is typically done in partnership with legal counsel. The key is to plan for it in advance so that junior staff are not trying to figure out what to do in the heat of the moment.

One final thought on escalation deals with how and when to involve legal counsel in both the preparation and the incident itself. There are several reasons for having legal counsel participate in the planning activities, developing communication plans, and being part of the escalation path. The primary objective is to minimize the organization's legal liability and maintain the organization's flexibility to participate in law enforcement actions or to pursue legal remedies. The legal group can:

- Identify the conditions that will trigger the notification of or escalation to law enforcement as well as the format of that notification

- Participate in crafting communications to minimize the organization's future liability

- Advise on contractual and regulatory implications and obligations of various containment and recovery options, such as the removal of files or the discontinuation (temporary or not, complete or not) of services

- Determine the nature and timing of disclosures, notably to regulators, when required

- Determine when it may be prudent to conduct deliberations about some or all of these options under the protection of privilege (e.g., in the anticipation of litigation)

Each member of the senior leadership team should understand their role in preparation activities, communication plans, escalation paths, and decision making. Cross training is also essential. Just as team members in all disciplines get sick and take vacations, so too you should assume that senior leaders are subject to unexpected unavailability.

Involve resources from key partners and suppliers to make sure the preparation includes the entire ecosystem, including key customers. Cyber incidents can involve assets associated not only with internal, back-office processes but often with customer-facing assets as well as assets that either require or contribute to partner networks and your technology supply chain or your customer's technology supply chain. For industries that are part of the nation's critical infrastructure, this could also involve government agencies and other partners in related companies. Assume that the incident will involve infrastructure not directly controlled by internal staff (e.g., shadow IT or from a service provider). As part of the overall incident response preparation, ask if there are any dependencies on third parties and how that dependency would affect a response.

The senior leadership team can help drive the engagement with partners and ensure that resources and priorities across organizational boundaries are aligned. Don't neglect key customers in preparation for cyber incidents. While some customers are more important from a revenue or reputation perspective, all customers should understand how the organization will communicate status, next steps, temporary service options, and expectations for service recovery. Larger, enterprise customers might have dedicated processes for informing them of incidents which may kick off formal response plans for them as well. Smaller customers or consumers may not be able to devote attention to your recovery plans until an incident impacts them.

As the company concludes eradication efforts and gains confidence that the affected systems are ready to resume business as usual, business process owners should begin to communicate service availability. A key aspect of that communication is informing everyone who needs to know how to recognize a repeat of the same attack. This is especially important if the initial attack vector relied on humans making mistakes. Usually, by this time, media coverage has subsided, but as an organization we still have customers who need assistance. If necessary, consider bringing on extra shift personnel for helpdesk activities and establish regular updates or alerts to the larger team.

The Purpose of Forensics

Assuming it is not engaged in combating nation-state actors, your organization will have two primary purposes for its forensics activities: preserving evidence for potential criminal investigation or civil litigation discovery and understanding your organization's vulnerabilities so that you can take additional preventive actions as warranted.

Preserving evidence is a mostly technical activity and the primary impact to the organization beyond the infrastructure and security teams will be patience while the business relies on backup or secondary systems so the physical or virtual systems that were compromised can be sequestered for evidentiary purposes. If the organization anticipates litigation resulting from an incident, it's critical to have counsel engage resources to support attorney-client privilege and work product scoped to support the investigation.

Identifying the vulnerabilities for your organization will require you to analyze the attack vector(s) that were used to gain access, the assets affected, the data extracted or other harms that were done, and the business processes that were impacted. Ensure that the team does not jump to conclusions too early in the process – the investigation should be thorough and look for the true root cause.

Post-Mortem Review

Now that the evidence has been collected and preserved and you have conducted your analysis, it is time to conduct the post-mortem review with your organization. The post-mortem is not monolithic. You should be flexible in your approach and tailor it to the type and scope of the incident. At the least, you should share your findings with your immediate team, your direct supervisor, and your peers.

Some incidents require a wider audience for the post-mortem. These include incidents with a wide-scale impact to internal processes or customer-facing processes. Also include incidents that were the result of or amplified by multiple human failures, such as the ubiquitous clicking on links from suspicious emails or text messages, sharing passwords, leaving passwords visible, or other actions you train your organization to avoid.

The post-mortem is most effective when pairing findings with actions. It might be cathartic or provide a sense of closure to identify the root cause, but unless you are just as forthcoming with the behaviors that need to change and the required actions, your workforce is not likely to make the changes necessary to avoid a repeat of the incident.

There are several questions that you should try to address with all audiences, but the exact framing you use will vary. In discussing how the organization prepares for incidents, you might share with the larger team that the curriculum will change to include more training on how to spot suspicious email or texts and how to report them to the help desk or security team. You'll want to include when to expect that instruction, what form it will take, and how you will measure success. With the management team, you would likely add details about how much it will cost to implement identified remediations.

Here are some of the questions you will want to address:

- Was the organization properly trained, and if not, what are the specific gaps to address?
- Were our communications appropriate?
- Did escalations occur timely and to the right individuals or departments?

- Are our technical capabilities, including staffing levels, staff skill sets, tools, and service providers, adequate to the required tasks?

- What was the total impact of this incident (be it operational, reputational, financial, or otherwise)?

- What corrective actions do we need to take?

- Did our analysis show that there were third parties, including enterprise software, that contributed, through inappropriate action or lack of action, and did we address that issue appropriately?

- How confident are we that the corrective actions we have taken give us reasonable assurance that we can prevent the same or a similar attack from occurring in the future?

IT and OT Convergence: The Game Has Changed

With the convergence of traditional IT and operational technology (OT), the potential impact on safety due to our technology footprint has never been more significant. We are beginning to see both physical harm and the loss of life resulting from cyber-attacks. Further, we will see liability claims against our organizations when we are negligent in our security and IT practices. Negligence and its implications are now part of our cybersecurity vocabulary.

We will also witness other significant changes resulting from this OT and IT convergence. Historically, software manufacturers sold, or more appropriately licensed, their software with near-absolute disclaimers of warranty. The software is typically licensed "AS IS" and "WITH ALL FAULTS." The Disclaimer of Warranty clauses found in most licensing agreements will also likely convey that there is no warranty that the software is free of defects or is suitable for any particular purpose. The software we use to run our organizations is laden with defects and flaws that challenge our efforts to secure our organizations, and we have limited to no recourse. These conditions will change.

Each year, the American Bar Association highlights some of the more prominent product liability cases, including a 2016/2017 case against Tesla related to purported software flaws in their Model X and Model S cars.[19] Tesla claims that it has no legal duty to create a fail-safe car. Nevertheless, Tesla actively solicits vulnerability reporting related to their vehicles.[20]

What we are witnessing is the significant, early change to "product liability" associated with software. One could argue, with techniques such as threat modeling and security by design principles and standards such as the Open Web Application Security Project's Application Security Verification Standard (OWASP ASVS), that these vulnerabilities could have been anticipated and addressed before being released to production.

These realities have a couple of important implications for our organizations. One is less dramatic than the other. First, when software manufacturers and organizations are held liable for software defects, there will be an inflationary event – software manufacturers will likely raise prices to address their financial exposure to product liability cases. Second, and at the heart of this chapter, how our organizations deal with security flaws – and the resulting incidents – have become the fodder of legal actions, media coverage, and the intense focus of the board of directors. Effectively, we are entering an era of increased liability and financial exposure resulting from the cybersecurity practices of our organization.

---

[19] Here are details related to this case:
http://www.abajournal.com/news/article/tesla_responds_to_lawsuit_by_claiming_it_has_no_duty_to_design_a_failsa.

[20] https://www.tesla.com/about/legal#security-vulnerability-reporting-policy

Having a discussion of negligence entails addressing the following topics:

- **Duty:** Given the number of regulations – both domestic and international – that require comprehensive security and privacy programs to be established, documenting a *legal duty of care* related to our security programs is all but guaranteed.

- **Breach of Duty:** With frameworks and standards establishing specific functions, capabilities, responsibilities, and the controls required for security programs, we've effectively moved from the cover of discretionary practices to prescriptive requirements and obligations.

- **Causation:** When an individual is harmed or injured as a result of a security patch not deployed timely, or a configuration setting provisioned incorrectly, there could be a case for establishing causation.

- **Damages:** With the conditions mentioned above, establishing a case for damages, e.g., liability and settlement awards could become likely.

Key Insights and Recommended Next Steps

We hope to have conveyed that preparation is the key to managing through cybersecurity incidents, be they isolated malware infestations or data breaches impacting thousands of customers with the potential to do great damage to the organization's reputation. Within our operational memory, we have experienced the effects of large-scale breaches and disruptive national events. Operational resilience is now expected and is achieved by the collective efforts of senior executives and the board, with the CISO playing a leading or key supporting role.

Balancing resource needs across competing objectives is a critical function of the board and a key requirement for effective governance. The board should take a lead role in ensuring that the organization is prepared to rapidly recover in the event of a disruption caused by cyber incidents and validate the preparations made to ensure business continuity. At the least, this would include allocating time on the board agenda to review plans and ask probing questions.

Preparation is key. Leadership must provide guidance for the communication plans and escalation paths, make sure that the communication plans appropriately deal with the situation, that they involve the right people in decision making, and that they deal with key concerns for employees, customers, shareholders, and concerned public officials such as law enforcement and regulators. Escalation paths are critical to being able to bring the situation under control rapidly. Frontline personnel need to know who to call, and under what circumstances to make that call. Senior management must ensure that the escalation path includes people at the correct level and with the proper skillset to make critical decisions for responding to the incident. Advanced preparation will allow the organization to quickly regain the narrative and de-escalate the issue.

Chapter 10

Executing the Cybersecurity Program

The best way to predict your future is to create it.

-Abraham Lincoln

Executive Summary

The temptation among those of us in the technical fields is to think of tools first. While tools are often helpful in solving various process problems, an over-reliance on tools is often expensive and usually decreases the effectiveness of any given program.

We recommend starting instead with a business impact analysis, asset inventory, and third-party risk assessment. These should provide an in-depth understanding of the organization's data assets and how this data flows into and out of the organization with third parties, processes, applications, and clients. Add to this continuity planning and an incident response plan to provide essential resilience.

Turnover and knowledge gaps create seams in the security program that leave the organization with blind spots and vulnerabilities. Essential to reducing turnover and closing knowledge gaps is continual skill development. Along with a well-trained and skilled security team, an effective awareness program is indispensable. An empowered workforce, confident in its ability to make good decisions, acts as both an early warning system and a shield.

Technical solutions will fall into two broad categories – tools used by the organization to deploy and maintain a secure infrastructure and tools used by the security organization to prevent bad events and monitor the network to expose questionable activities for follow up.

Your organization faces a dynamic threat environment that is continually evolving. New threats will at times require changes to security controls and the technology used to execute these controls and the cybersecurity budget must be flexible enough to accommodate the occasional urgent need. Budgets that are too tight to begin with or overloaded with long-term commitments may force decisions made for budgetary reasons that are not in the best interest of securing critical assets. Tying all of this spending together is the strategic plan.

Start with Knowledge About the Business

By now it should come as no surprise that tools and techniques for CISOs and their security teams is near the end of our discussion. We've emphasized the importance of understanding the business processes and assets we're protecting, the threat landscape in which we operate, the value of a well-trained workforce aware of and committed to their role, and how essential resilient business processes are to resisting and recovering from business interruptions in general and cyber incidents in particular. Now we're going to describe how these elements fit together into a comprehensive cybersecurity program.

We'll get to tools in a bit, but for now, we're going to skip the laundry list of cybersecurity offerings…all completely new, powered by AI, and backed by venture capital. There is no shortage of options, and when the organization has clearly defined requirements and approaches the evaluation, purchase, installation, and configuration judiciously, there is good reason to expect that the selected tools will have a positive impact on securing the enterprise and its data. But there is a lot that should be done before drafting an RFP.

Let's start by acknowledging that you cannot secure something you don't know exists. An asset inventory that includes physical assets, data assets, and virtual assets is a critical first step. It is also an essential way for the CISO to get to a ground truth as it can tie directly to the organization's finance and accounting departments – most assets should appear in a fixed asset ledger, on an operational budget for items such as software licensing, or on an invoice or manifest from a cloud vendor. Additionally, for many organizations today, the most precious assets are their information and data. The compromise of this data is also the most significant potential liability for these organizations, especially for organizations that handle ePHI, PII, or cardholder data.

Next, there are few exercises more essential (and, sadly, more often overlooked) than a Business Impact Analysis (BIA). As we mentioned in Chapters 6 and 9, BIAs provide the essential linkages between business processes (and their value to the organization) and the underlying dependencies – be they with third parties or IT infrastructure. Essential elements of a BIA include potential loss scenarios given various causes, such as disasters, supplier disruptions, or cyber incidents, and these form the foundation of any risk assessment. In addition to lost sales and increased expenses, the potential impact on customers and operations, along with fines, regulatory sanctions, and contractual penalties, feed directly into recovery prioritization.

The artifact of the BIA is just a document or spreadsheet. The value of doing the BIA is that it necessitates knowledge of the organization's business (processes, vendors, and customers). Obtaining this knowledge requires the CISO to work collaboratively with other departments and executives within the organization. We cannot overstate the return on investment for this "tool."

As a subset of the BIA, another assessment that is required is a list of material third parties and their risk profiles. Given the number of high-profile breaches involving third-party relationships, there should be no ambiguity about the impact third parties can have on security. Critical in this effort is an understanding of what type of data we share with third parties, and which processes they support. Chapter 3 provides excellent context on third-party risk.

The results of the BIA and third-party risk assessment should provide a more in-depth understanding of the organization's data assets and how this data flows into and out of the organization with third parties, processes, applications, and clients. Knowing how data moves inside and outside the organization provides invaluable context for the types of security controls that may be required (e.g., access control lists, rule sets related to ports and processes, encryption, and user access rights).

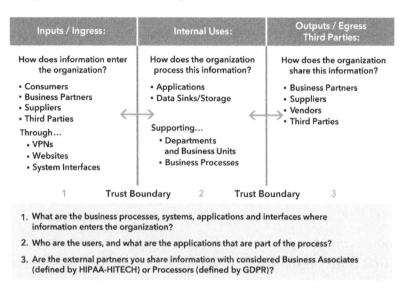

Figure 10.1 High-level depiction of Trust Boundaries[21]

The artifact of this data flow analysis is the data flow diagram (DFD). DFDs should capture the starting, transactional, and ending phases of a process or procedure. They should also clearly capture applications, organizational boundaries, people, roles, departments, data sets, and locations, among other variables. DFDs should document how information enters the organization, how it is processed internally (business processes, applications, and IT infrastructure) as well as how it is shared with third parties. In the chart above, the left column is where information is ingested, the middle column represents internal uses of the information, and the right column represents where the information is shared. The lines are effectively trust boundaries that should be reviewed from a security control perspective.

---

[21] This table is reproduced from Chapter 8 of the *CISO Desk Reference Guide, Volume 1, 2nd Edition*, CISO DRG Publishing – Bonney, Hayslip & Stamper

The results of the asset inventory, BIA, vendor assessment, and DFD documentation should inform the types of controls and procedures that will have the most impact on the security and governance of the organization. These are typically captured and described in the security policies. This data, business process, and vendor context can also be used to provide insights into threat modeling exercises.

None of these techniques require specialized tools or significant budget. What they do need is the commitment of the CISO to have an in-depth working knowledge of the organization, its industry, and its information and data, coupled with strong working relationships with colleagues across departments and divisions within the organization.

Another critical input to any discussion about security tools and controls is the organization's threat intel program. In Chapter 8 we talk about situational awareness. Specifically, knowing your industry, your employees and key stakeholders, your organization's processes, the applications that support these processes, and the underlying infrastructure (operating systems, hardware, and networks). The other two topics explored in Chapter 8, monitoring and continuity planning, are both informed by the environment in which the organization operates. Which tools you choose to rely on for monitoring depends partly on what you are monitoring.

Invest in People

In Chapter 7 we write about the human element. The next three tools we have come to rely on focus on our people. Turnover and knowledge gaps create seams in the security program that leave the organization with blind spots and vulnerabilities. Essential to reducing turnover and closing knowledge gaps is investing in the security team by focusing on good hiring practices and continual training for skill development.

Along with a well-trained and skilled security team, an effective awareness program is indispensable. An empowered workforce, confident in its ability to make good decisions, acts as both an early warning system and a shield that stops some fault lines from forming. Coupled with the cyber drills conducted as part of the incident response preparation, the workforce becomes a security force multiplier rather than just a large number of walking vulnerabilities.

An important component of the awareness program includes security policies. Policies are another tool we use to ground the workforce and decision makers in sound practices. Well-crafted security policies that are measured for effectiveness help the team distinguish between safe behavior and risky behavior and fill in the gaps for what is not covered in the awareness training.

Ben Franklin is famous for many things, including the adage, "An ounce of prevention is worth more than a pound of cure." It's often cited in connection with disease prevention, but he was instead referring to fire prevention and was trying to get the fire brigade in his adopted city of Philadelphia to embrace the fire prevention techniques he had recently come upon in Boston. In that spirit, the business continuity plan we discussed in Chapter 8 as well as the incident response planning that we discussed throughout this book, starting in Chapter 1, are key weapons in the CISO's arsenal. Not only will the process of creating these plans provide key insights for prevention and recovery and allow for crucial linkages between the security team and the functional units and lines of business, having these plans in place before the incident occurs is critical for a timely recovery.

Prevention begets resilience. Resilience also comes from redundancy, a sound foundation, and regular upkeep. To that end, recovery often relies on a robust backup strategy, which is a critical part of the continuity plan. Like building an asset inventory, performing a business impact analysis, and developing a data flow diagram, working with the organization to understand the backup strategy provides additional data points for the CISO about critical assets and priorities for recovery. A sound foundation is one designed with structural safety in mind. Configuration management and orchestration allow you to decrease the number of defects that make their way into the infrastructure from the time it is first deployed and as it is operated. Fewer defects mean fewer vulnerabilities and after poor access controls, exploiting vulnerabilities is the greatest attack vector. Even with golden, secure configurations faithfully copied, new vulnerabilities are constantly being discovered and exploited, which makes the case for adding vulnerability management, patch management, and penetration testing to our list of critical tools.

Be Strategic with Your Tools

Security teams have thousands of tools produced by hundreds of vendors to choose from. The tools they choose to deploy will fit broadly into three categories: preventive, detective, and corrective.

We'll start with preventive tools. But even in this context, when we say tools, we mean both tools and controls, not just pieces of hardware or software to buy or license. Access controls fit into this category. Security will work with IT and the businesses to limit both who has access to which assets (for example, role- and attribute-based controls and least privilege) and how assets are configured and what other assets they have access to (for instance, defining access control lists). By limiting the actions of people and the various applications and infrastructure, we cut down on unnecessary and often unsafe traffic. In effect, we are also limiting the damage that can be done. If an individual's account is compromised or an application has been compromised and is behaving in an unsafe manner, limited access results in a limited sphere of damage. Other access controls, such as VPNs and multi-factor authentication, are essential as well.

Limiting the damage is increasingly achieved by adopting a zero trust approach that assumes every endpoint (or resource) cannot be trusted. In a sense, we assume that every endpoint is a threat, limit each endpoint's access, verify each resource before granting access, and log all activity on the network. Zero trust assumes there is no implicit trust granted to assets or user accounts based solely on their physical or network location (i.e., local area networks versus the internet) or based on asset ownership (enterprise or personally owned).

In addition to access controls, security will deploy solutions that protect endpoints and servers from viruses and other malware and will also filter email. As we mentioned earlier, the number one attack vector is email, so filtering email is critical. Another important control is to have a thoughtful encryption strategy focused on network traffic carrying sensitive data. In some circumstances, encryption can also offer sanctuary from certain regulatory reporting requirements.

It's difficult to find an organization that doesn't support wireless access (on-premises) and remote access for a wide range of workers, and the configurations for these solutions need to be rigorously set up and monitored. Finally, network firewalls and web application firewalls should be deployed using a layered approach. Firewalls should never be a one and done option. Like access control lists, firewalls should be used to enforce trust boundaries to create a layered defense. Depending on the industry and technology footprint, there may be additional preventive controls the organization will choose to deploy.

The next category is tools that perform a detective function. In Chapter 8 we detailed several conditions and events that security teams should monitor. Some of these serve a threat intel purpose, such as monitoring the dark web for chatter about the company, but most constitute real and potential indicators of compromise. These include your current vulnerabilities, scanning, and activity directed at you.

We talked above about the importance of configuration management tools and monitoring the drift from approved baselines to what is actually deployed is an important data point for looming trouble. This should be done using automated tools with a sufficient frequency to detect assets that could have a short life span because ethereal assets are a hallmark of cloud-based deployment strategies. Also included in this category are intrusion detection tools that monitor traffic inside your network (physical or virtual) for unexpected activity. And finally, coordinating many of these solutions would be a security information and event management (SIEM) system. As with preventive tools and controls, there are additional tools or flavors of these tools that should be considered and are often deployed in combination. As always, each situation is different and the tools that any organization deploys should be calibrated to solve their unique problem set.

Corrective tools and controls, whether manual or automated, allow the organization to act based on an unwanted condition or event. For example, some configuration management tools can trigger a revert to approved configuration and some access control tools can trigger the automatic disabling of accounts or privileges that violate approved access rights. In many cases, the corrective action needs to be manually initiated based on the output of monitoring tools, and corrective capabilities are built into the monitoring tools. Whichever way the orchestration is set up, the key is to make sure that corrective action is appropriate and timely, and the need for corrective action becomes a monitoring point on its own.

Budget and Strategic Plan

The final two tools we rely on are the cybersecurity budget and the strategic plan. Your organization faces a dynamic threat environment that is continually evolving. New threats will at times require changes to security controls and the technology used to execute these controls and the cybersecurity budget must be flexible enough to accommodate the occasional urgent need. When this is caused by the organization exploring a new business opportunity, the immediate need for new tooling should be part of the start-up cost, but this will eventually need to be worked into the operating budget for security. Budgets that are too tight to begin with or overloaded with long-term commitments may force decisions made for budgetary reasons that are not in the best interest of securing critical assets. Tying all of this spending together is the strategic plan.

The strategic plan should encapsulate the mission and vision so that both security personnel and the workforce at large understand how the security function supports the organization's goals and objectives. The security function often performs a critical governance function over controls and data protection and therefore should have its own governance spelled out, so it is clear how the organization knows that the security function is successfully achieving its goals. A set of strategic objectives, arrayed over a one- to three-year timeline, should lay out how the cybersecurity organization will invest its time and resources to manage the organization's security risks. A series of time-bound key initiatives would then detail the actions to be taken to achieve the strategic objectives.

Key Insights and Recommended Next Steps

We said in Chapter 1 that organizations are demanding more of their CISOs. We stated that they expect their CISOs to move beyond their in-depth technical knowledge and offer domain expertise in the areas of risk management and business operations. The specific area where we believe CISOs can add value is in building resilience and agility into the fabric of the company. A company's ability to rebound quickly from an incident, whether it is a natural disaster or a cyber incident, is a strategic advantage. So too, resilience in the face of long-term disruptions, such as climate change, will be a critical survival skill for organizations.

When offices had to close due to the COVID-19 global pandemic, many companies discovered that changes they thought were impossible, such as support for large-scale remote work, were in fact possible. CISOs were essential to implementing work-from-home models securely and in allowing companies to evolve work-from-home into work-from-anywhere and remote-first models. This demonstrated ability to implement a new workforce paradigm quickly and securely will be a model for other changes to operations that are thought to be beyond our abilities. In other words, the demands on the business to be far more agile in the face of change are now baked into expectations for successful leaders.

As you can see from our list of tools and techniques, a CISO relies on much more than widgets they can buy. In addition to the strategic implementation of technology, they rely on an in-depth knowledge of the organization, they rely on the entire organization's workforce, they rely on thorough preparation, strategic thinking, and budgeting, and most of all, they rely on their human network.

As the first step in the cybersecurity strategic plan, we recommend the CISO, senior leadership team, and board validate the organization's business impact analysis, asset inventory, third-party risk assessment, continuity plan, and incident response plan.

Chapter 11

Management and the Board

Eloquence is the power to translate a truth into language perfectly intelligible to the person to whom you speak

~Ralph Waldo Emerson

Executive Summary

The inclusion of cybersecurity as an agenda item for board meetings has grown dramatically since the watershed Target breach of 2013. The quick succession of other breaches, including Home Depot, Wyndham, and JP Morgan Chase, put boards on notice. More recent events, such as the SolarWinds breach in 2020 and the Microsoft Exchange Server attack and the Colonial Pipeline ransomware attack in 2021, have made the point that boards must understand cyber risk inescapable. Guidance for boards on this subject is available from multiple resources, including the Securities and Exchange Commission, the National Association of Corporate Directors (NACD), and regulatory bodies such as the Federal Financial Institutions Examination Council (FFIEC).

At a minimum, boards should consider the following areas of ongoing concern:

- **Evaluation of incident response capabilities**
  The board should provide oversight of the organization's preparedness to deal with cybersecurity incidents and the board's unique role in the response and aftermath.

- **Review and authorization of budgets**
  The board should ensure that an appropriate budget is made available to address cybersecurity priorities and that allocated funds are deployed to good outcomes.

- **Adequacy of insurance**
  The board should have confidence that cyber liability insurance is in place to transfer appropriate risk through contracts, including adequate funds and assistance for ongoing operations and recovery to a pre-incident state.

- **Ensuring organizational accountability**

The board should verify that management has appropriate internal and external reviews of decisions and actions.

- **Evaluation and assessment of controls and disclosures**
  The board should validate that required controls have been implemented, and that management is appropriately monitoring and disclosing performance.

While the board and the CISO are both concerned with risk, the language and vernacular used may be quite different. Throughout the ongoing communications between the board, executive management, and the CISO, all parties should strive for clarity and ideally incorporate core enterprise risk management principles into proceedings.

The Board's Unique Role

Let's take a moment to think about the role of the board of directors as it pertains to cybersecurity. Boards are elected (or in certain organizations appointed) to represent the true stakeholders in an organization. The board is expected to exercise its collective duties of oversight and due care, review the strategy, planning, and execution of executive management, and guide its strategy and address organizational risks.

The inclusion of cybersecurity as an agenda item for board meetings has grown dramatically since the watershed Target breach of 2013. Many derivative lawsuits that were ultimately unsuccessful focused on Target's board of directors and questioned whether they fulfilled their oversight and due care obligations. The quick succession of other breaches, including Home Depot, Wyndham, and JP Morgan Chase, put boards on notice. The spate of ransomware attacks impacting organizations globally has only intensified the board's interest in cyber risk. Moreover, many individual board members have been the victims of spear-phishing and other social engineering attacks – generating additional impetus to understand how secure the organizations they serve actually are.

There is also critical context from the SEC. In October 2011, the SEC issued disclosure guidance related to cybersecurity risk. It noted that detail related explicitly to material cyber risks and breaches should be captured in one or more of the following sections of the annual or quarterly report: risk factors, management's discussion and analysis (MD&A), description of the business, legal proceedings, financial statement disclosures, and disclosure controls and procedures. Additionally, organizations are expected to disclose material changes to the organization's cyber risk profile in current reports filed on Forms 8-K. Implicit in the SEC's guidance is a requirement for both executive management, notably the CEO and

CFO, and the board of directors to truly understand the risk implications of a cyber incident or breach.

In February 2018, the SEC clarified expectations relative to cybersecurity risk and appropriate disclosures. The "Commission Statement and Guidance on Public Company Cybersecurity Disclosures" expanded upon the 2011 guidance to require management to understand the financial implications – notably around remediation – of a breach. The bottom line is that boards and executive management are now fully on notice that the cybersecurity practices and the quality of their organization's security program warrant their attention.

The Board Is Now a Target

Whether because of shareholder derivative suits aimed at specific board members, comments from the SEC, or guidance from external advisors and auditors on the subject, the topic of cybersecurity is on the agenda for most boards. While boards are now more interested than ever in cybersecurity and cyber risk management, there are still important considerations that impact the effectiveness of the board's fiduciary oversight of an organization's cyber risk tolerance.

Cybersecurity is a challenging topic for many board members, new in its implications to the organization and distinct in its vocabulary and technology. Board members know that they should be concerned and exercise due care and oversight. Still, they may lack the knowledge, context, or even basic cyber vocabulary to competently address the issue. This lack of experience is one reason we are seeing new board structures being developed to either expand the charter of the audit committee or create a separate risk committee whose charter includes cybersecurity. Regardless of the organizational structure, the board will need to develop cyber acumen and consider appointing a qualified technical executive

(QTE) to help the board assess management's cybersecurity practices and management's evaluation and treatment of cyber-related risk.

Guidance for Boards

Fortunately, there is actionable and prescriptive guidance to help boards effectively oversee cyber for their organizations. This guidance comes from multiple resources ranging from the SEC to the Digital Directors Network (DDN) and the National Association of Corporate Directors (NACD), regulatory agencies such as the Federal Financial Institutions Examination Council (FFIEC), and legal counsel, advisory services, and other sources. Collectively, the recommendations are consistent in their tone and practicality. Let's summarize these into a list of board requirements that a CISO can facilitate and support.

Boards should expect CISOs to tailor their presentations to the board's preferences. Most boards will likely prefer summarized information versus technical detail on the issues listed below. The effective CISO will adjust their communications to suit their audience. As a general rule of thumb, the CISO should translate overly technical material into higher-level business impact or enterprise risk management context. Vulnerabilities in "Apache Struts" won't resonate with the board...the effects on enterprise value will.

Evaluation of Incident Response Capabilities

Boards should be aware of their organization's capabilities to respond to a cyber incident or a breach. While the board may not be expected to read the full incident response plan in detail, they will want to know that the incident response plan exists, that it's been tested (and the results of this testing), and the role of executive management in implementing the plan effectively. CISOs should provide an overview of incident response capabilities, requirements for additional resources to support incident response, and an escalation matrix that includes designated members of the board in the event of a breach, a widespread ransomware attack affecting operations, or another cyber-related matter that puts the organization at material risk.

- **Counsel** – The board should know the role of the organization's legal counsel in handling incident response. For many organizations, the first call following the discovery of a cyber incident (be it a data breach or a ransomware attack) should be to counsel to invoke attorney-client privilege and facilitate communication with regulatory and law enforcement officials. Boards, the executive leadership team, and the CISO should be aware that privilege requires special labeling of communications and that counsel's guidance can only be protected with privilege where there is anticipation of litigation. Communications with regulators and law enforcement, while confidential, may not be considered privileged communications.[22] CISOs, with the guidance and support of the extended executive team, should have these procedures documented and tested.

- **Regulatory and law enforcement** – The board will also need to know how law enforcement and regulators are to be engaged depending upon the nature and extent of the incident. These are procedures that should be routinely practiced by using tabletop exercises and other methods to ensure the executive team is prepared.

- **Notifications and escalation** – A basic RACI matrix should be provided to the board that includes the board itself and

---

[22] The case of the Capital One breach and the work product and attorney-client privilege warrants a review: https://www.mofo.com/resources/insights/200608-data-breach-incident.html

details how notifications and escalations should be triaged when an event occurs. The last thing that anyone wants to do during an incident is to determine under fire whom to notify. A breach is an eventuality that should be anticipated and documented within the incident response plan. Don't leave anything to ambiguity and clarify understandings and expectations with stakeholders.

Review and Authorization of Budgets

Boards have an important role in reviewing the overall budget of the organization. Part of their assessment is to ensure that the organization ties funding of critical cyber-related functions to the organization's strategy. Unfortunately, organizations frequently see cybersecurity as a cost to the organization rather than a business or process enabler, and further, fail to provide adequate funding for risk reduction. Even under the best of circumstances, organizations view cybersecurity as something analogous to an insurance premium – begrudgingly paid, with an emphasis on spending the least amount possible. The board needs to work closely with their CISO – and with executive management – to ensure that the cyber budget is tied to the organization's overall risk appetite. A review of budget adequacy and the funding of critical cyber activities in the context of contractual and regulatory obligations is prudent. The board should note whether there are material risks that are either under-resourced or under-funded, and whether that status is understood by key stakeholders.

Adequacy of Insurance

Insurance is a significant risk treatment vehicle. Cyber liability insurance is a vital tool for mitigating financial exposure following a breach. Expenses after a breach may include tangible costs such as penalties and fines, consumer notifications and credit monitoring, legal expenses, and hardware repair or replacement, as well as intangible costs, including damage to an organization's reputation. The organization's opportunity cost as critical staff is focused on incident response and clean up rather than their normal responsibilities is also a factor. The board and executive management should enlist the CISO to evaluate the adequacy of the cyber-liability coverage and facilitate the application process. The scourge of ransomware has changed the cyber liability insurance market and premiums have increased notably over the last several years.

Ensuring Organizational Accountability

The board should know who is ultimately accountable for cybersecurity within the organization. Board members are ill-served if their oversight is limited because they do not have access to – or much worse, knowledge of – the leader who oversees cybersecurity within the organization. Under ideal circumstances, the board should have unfettered access to the CISO, and there should be routine, calendared updates on all items related to cyber. As noted in the incident response section above, a basic RACI matrix is an essential first step in this regard. CISOs should not define organizational risk tolerances. The board and executive management should define this. It's the CISO's role to validate whether the current security program can meet acceptable risk objectives.

Evaluation and Assessment of Controls and Disclosures

The SEC's guidance, coupled with other recommendations from board-focused groups, clearly suggests that boards need to develop a level of cyber acumen to ensure their ability to provide competent oversight.[23] There are analogies to other functional disciplines that

---

[23] There is growing attention on ensuring that boards have digitally literate members, including board members with security knowledge. One organization,

will put this objective in context. Following the scandals of Enron and Arthur Andersen, the Sarbanes-Oxley Act emphasized the board's role in overseeing financial reporting controls and disclosures. The audit committee's role within the board took on greater importance, and the requirement for its members to have financial reporting and accounting competencies grew significantly. Today we see an emphasis on developing technology and cyber-related skills within boards. The board of directors should contract with third-party resources to facilitate their evaluation of security practices within their organization if these skills are not readily available in existing board members.

Boards will need to evaluate the effectiveness in both design and operation of the organization's security controls as wells as its security policies, procedures, and other practices. The board should also have a level of understanding regarding the types of assets (be they physical or logical) that would be impacted by a failure of cybersecurity controls. They should understand how these failures should be made known to the markets and the organization's customers, regulators, and other stakeholders. Again, this is a compelling reason for the board to assess incident response plans and activities. The board should work with the CISO to evaluate the relative knowledge of cybersecurity associated with their executive management colleagues and the board and help facilitate cyber awareness and training.

The Unique Role of the CISO

Senior leadership and boards require that the CISO is capable of being the external face of the company in some circumstances, to lend credibility to the organization and create confidence in successful outcomes. The communication role, in this case, is mostly with regulators and auditors. The regulators and auditors' goals are

---

the Digital Directors Network, is advocating greater cyber knowledge should be a requisite for boards.

to assess the organization's commitment to and management's competence at creating successful programs to ensure compliance. Technical acumen, integrity, and consistency in action are being tested, and again, clear, concise communications are essential. While it is at times necessary for CISOs to demonstrate mastery of the subject, including the standards and compliance requirements, it is not expected that they provide a significant level of detail. Other than remedial plans for addressing deficiencies, CISOs should leave the technical deep dives for the direct staff.

One of the first tasks for the CISO will be to clearly define their role and the roles of their peers and the entire executive leadership team in incident response. They will need to create a response plan early and practice it often, so it doesn't need to be invented on the fly.

Key to success in incident management is to keep communications timely and consistent and hit on these three themes: "what happened," "what's the impact," and "what are we doing about it." Keep to the facts. It is especially important to keep speculation to an absolute minimum. The CISO should instruct their teams to avoid using language that may require disclosure (e.g., data breach) in their internal communications, notably in ticketing systems. Procedures for declaring an incident, and most importantly a data breach, should be validated by the CISO and the organization's counsel. Remember that nature abhors a vacuum. If your organization fails to provide a narrative about what transpired, the impact, and your reaction, one will be provided for you.

Cybersecurity risk is as significant to the business as risks posed by strategic, operational, financial, or compliance operations to corporate boards. For the board, providing effective oversight of cybersecurity risk means the difference between learning about cybersecurity after a breach with significant damages and having a mature cybersecurity program that can mitigate the costs of a breach with minimal exposure to the company. In today's fast-moving business environment, boards can't claim a lack of awareness as a defense against allegations of improper or inadequate oversight. Boards of directors and executive management must educate themselves about cybersecurity and the risk exposure of their organizations. This knowledge is crucial; it enables board members to make strategic decisions with a full understanding of how cyber risk impacts their business plans.

Tone at the Top

Ultimately, boards represent and function as the voice of the stakeholders of the organization. Proactive and well-informed boards can set the all-important tone at the top and have a strong influence on the organization's operational effectiveness. CISOs should know their organization's board members, their respective roles on the board, and their fundamental interests.

With that as background, we can now focus on the CISO's role with the executive management team. Three key concepts to consider are the CISO's role within the organization, each person or group's role in the current conversation, and the desired outcome from each interaction. Keeping these concepts top of mind will help the CISO deliver the message in an easy-to-consume form with a definite next step, grounded in understandable and relevant consequences to the organization.

Let's start at the outcome and work back. By outcome, we mean what needs to be accomplished. Consider whether the purpose is to inform, to collaborate, or to trigger a call to action. It is critical to be clear about the desired outcome to achieve concise and specific communications.

When the CISO addresses the board or the executive management team, the story needs to have a beginning, middle, and end. It also needs to be interesting and should have a goal. Some examples:

1. *Inform and Educate* – convey that leveraging a new technology provides opportunities. However, it also exposes new risks that must be addressed.

2. *Influence a Decision* – make a case for why a specific action should be taken. For example, the cybersecurity program should be moved out of the IT department to address "segregation of duties" issues.

3. *Change Behavior* – show how a current organizational process, behavior, or standard opens the organization up to unacceptable risk. Demonstrate workable alternatives that will reduce risk exposure with minimal impact on business operations.

Inform

Is this a routine update about ongoing efforts to drive the cybersecurity program? Did a peer, or the CEO, or a member of the board ask for an opinion or a status update on an investigation, remediation, or deployment effort? Is this a warning to management or colleagues about impending problems that will impact their agendas? These different questions can be handled in ways ranging from a simple verbal response to an interactive dashboard. The fundamental principles are to use business terms and state business impact. Stay away from jargon and technical consequences. Especially when the purpose is informational, and there is no immediate call to action, consider providing a small number (one to three) of key takeaways. Think: "If they get nothing more from this report, they should know this."

Routine communications, such as dashboards, report cards, and project status, should be as consistent as possible. They should always note changes, such as dropping or adding specific metrics. The goal for these routine vehicles is to "quickly inform." There can be detail "one click down," but the audience has limited bandwidth for the domain, so the presentation should do the work for them; ensure that they can easily find the key message(s).

Collaborate

Is this a strategy or planning session? Is the CISO's participation routine, or is it a one-time or probationary appearance? What is the CISO's role – expert, colleague, or business leader? Regardless of the expectations communicated, the CISO must always be prepared to be the security expert. This preparation is essential for maintaining the trust that management places in the CISO and the information security department.

Another necessary collaboration skill for the CISO is to leverage management and the board to build the human network needed to be effective in the role. As with all interactions at this level, a specific call to action is more effective than a general request. The CISO should learn to ask for help and ask for introductions and support where required. The primary goals here are to solve problems, grow in the field, broaden the skill set, and develop cohesion in the management team. By integrating better with these critical leaders, the CISO improves their personal and professional network, which can help them solve problems when expertise outside of the direct network is needed.

One final aspect of collaboration is the responsibility to teach. This manifests itself through teaching the information security team and those directly responsible for technical deployments. But it also includes teaching at the executive level. The messages should be simple. The audience is people who are often not in the technical domain and have a lot on their plate. The messages should be focused on what the extended leadership team needs to communicate with their stakeholders.

Call to Action

Is an action to be taken based on the information being provided? What is the purpose and timeframe of that action? What are the consequences of acting and not acting? Which resources will be required and when?

Like having key takeaways from purely informational interactions, the necessary actions must rise to the top any time you call for action. Don't overwhelm the audience with too many high-priority activities. While the CISO's objective for a "full-frontal assault" might be to "light a fire," the result is often a feeling of helplessness followed inevitably by paralysis. To avoid this overwhelming and numbing effect, consider "grading on a curve." By showing relative performance, management's attention can be focused on the most significant problems or the lowest hanging fruit.

Cybersecurity tactical issues are not likely to occupy much time for the board or executive management, with one notable exception. We have entered the era of celebrity vulnerabilities and high-profile breaches, notably highly publicized ransomware attacks. It is becoming common for boards and senior management to ask how a particular vulnerability affects the organization or if the most recent high-profile breach can happen to us. The CISO needs to provide concise answers that quickly and truthfully demonstrate mastery of the issue and relate it to their organization. If this vulnerability or the techniques used to cause that breach pose a real threat, make sure the board knows why, what is being done about it, and how they can help.

To Whom Am I Speaking?

Next, the CISO should focus on the role of the individual or group with whom they are communicating. While the essence of the message is unchanged, how that message is framed might be very different. One of the frequent complaints about interacting with

CISOs is that they are often mired in detail or use technical language or jargon that is difficult to decipher. Being aware of the audience's natural filters is essential to useful communications.

Business leaders are apt to be concerned with the impact on their operations. Do they need to pivot on their strategy based on what you are saying? Do they need to take immediate remedial action? Do they need to account for new information in planning? How will this impact their sales or customer service? The CEO might be more interested in the impact across divisions, employee morale, market impact, or public scrutiny. The board, along with the CEO, would be interested in the effects on company strategy, public scrutiny, regulatory implications, and any liability you explicitly or implicitly list.

The factual basis of the message doesn't change. But by being mindful of the audience, the CISO will be better positioned to provide the information the recipient needs to fulfill their role.

Now that the purpose of the audience is known, it is time to focus on the CISO's role at the moment. The CISO needs to be aware of their stated and unstated role in the organization. What is the organization relying on the CISO to do? Is it a mostly technical role? Does the organization expect the CISO to tell them when things are not secure, and why? Is the role more focused on business resilience, business acumen, or perhaps the chief technology BS detector? Is the key contribution a successful compliance outcome (including staying out of regulatory trouble), breach detection, breach prevention, public relations, or public/regulatory or customer confidence? As tempting as it is to declare that the role is all of the above, knowing the role relative to the specific situation will allow the message to be targeted at the right outcome.

Guidance and Direction on Risk Management

Along with executive management, boards play an integral role in overseeing risk management for the organization. Board members have a fiduciary responsibility to understand the risk environment and provide guidance on the organization's risk-treatment strategy. The board's risk management perspective extends beyond cyber to include operational, financial, reputational, and other enterprise risk management considerations.

There are some practical analyses that the CISO can provide to the board to assist them in evaluating risk. Ideally, the CISO will do this in collaboration with other members of the executive team, with the CISO playing a leading role in communicating detail and status on the following:

- **Organizational assets** – The CISO, with support from other colleagues, should provide a list of assets that require due care, including the firm's intellectual property (IP), key data sets such as protected health information, cardholder data, and core processes. To keep this information meaningful, a CISO might leverage a high-level data flow diagram to show the board the linkages between organizational assets, information, staff, and third parties leveraged by the organization that could impact risk treatment.

- **Risk assessment** – The CISO should draft an overall cyber risk assessment for the organization. The risk assessment should take a holistic view of cyber to include third parties, systems, applications, personnel, and data. Provide a summary of the risk factors and their recommended treatment to the board and executive management at least twice a year, and certainly following any material changes to the organization's operating environment. The use of a trusted third party to facilitate this assessment may also be necessary to ensure credibility.

- **Suppliers and third parties** – CISOs can play an important role in quantifying the risk of third parties, independent contractors, and service providers. Documenting these dependencies in a board-friendly manner is a valuable exercise.

- **Threat landscape** – Boards are concerned about many risk factors facing the organization, including changes to the industry, regulations, new competitors, and changes to the executive team. The board must also be aware of the threat landscape facing the organization's systems, applications, and IT infrastructure. A CISO can provide quarterly updates summarizing these changes in the threat landscape and relating them to the organization's industry or another context.

Executive management teams and boards, especially those of publicly traded companies (where comparable information is often more available), leverage comparisons and baselining as a tool to oversee the performance of the organization. Financial ratios help management determine how well the organization is performing, the effectiveness of its use of capital, and whether the company is heading in the right direction in general. Boards relish an opportunity to compare and contrast. CISOs should detail how the organization compares to such key frameworks and standards as the NIST Cybersecurity Framework, COBIT, ISO, or other recognized approaches to cybersecurity management. Every organization has its challenges, so a CISO should convey the ground truth to the board. If specific key controls or activities are ineffective, the board should know. Helping the board develop a comfort level with basic security

Management and the Board

metrics is an essential element in successful board and executive management communication.

CISOs should help the board baseline security spending relative to the organization's industry and other risk variables, including the cost of a breach. Does the organization have the right cybersecurity capabilities to address its specific threat landscape? Are the staffing levels and competencies sufficient for the work at hand, and can the organization adequately address third-party risk? CISOs should help the board understand the cybersecurity budget and make recommendations that lower overall security costs for the organization while still providing adequate protection. CISOs should also provide a detailed review of their options and preferences if more budget were available.

CISOs who are aware of the board's fiduciary responsibilities and the motivations of executive management concerning cybersecurity will be more effective in advocating for their requirements when they tailor their communications and status updates to these two audiences. CISOs that translate cybersecurity into the governance and oversight language used by the board will find that their insights, perspectives, and requirements will be listened to and acted upon in a spirit of mutual collaboration.

Key Insights and Recommended Next Steps

Boards are elected to represent the true stakeholders in an organization. For publicly traded companies, these are shareholders. The board is expected to exercise its duties of oversight and due care and review the strategy, planning, and execution of executive management and to guide the organization's risk strategies. For executives with little experience communicating with the board, this can be an intimidating prospect, and it might be challenging to capture the critical points at the right level.

Though cybersecurity is an evolving and complex topic, it is no less critical to the organization than other topics the board oversees. As the lead cybersecurity professional for the organization, the CISO should project competence and professionalism.

To build credibility, the CISO should function on the executive team as a trusted teammate. To that end, a key mantra should be "No Surprises!" The CISO is the center of an ecosystem – creating metrics to measure the cybersecurity program's effectiveness, producing and managing dashboards to execute strategy, and reporting on the maturity of the control environment to executive management. Effective strategies that will assist the CISO in formulating their narrative include demonstrating alignment with the organization's strategic plans, using common industry benchmarks to allow for comparisons with peer companies, and using data to create an objective assessment.

It is crucial for the CISO to not just champion the cybersecurity program to stakeholders but also understand how the company operates and what changes are needed to align the cybersecurity strategy to its overall business goals.

Bibliography

What follows is a non-traditional bibliography composed of references from this book as well as several other books in the CISO Desk Reference Guide catalog.

Articles and Books on Talent Management, Risk, Data Classification, and Security Controls

(FS-ISAC), F. S. (2019). *Home.* Retrieved from https://www.fsisac.com/
(SIFMA), S. I. (2019). *Cybersecurity Resources.* Retrieved from
    https://www.sifma.org/cybersecurity-resources/
Adler, S. (2007, May 31). *CIO Magazine.* Retrieved from CIO Magazine
    Website: http://www.cio.com/article/2438861/enterprise-
    architecture/six-steps-to-data-governance-success.html
AICPA. (2019). *SOC for Service Organizations.* Retrieved from
    https://www.aicpa.org/interestareas/frc/assuranceadvisoryservices/aicpas
    oc2report.html
Alliance, N. C. (2019). *CyberSecure My Business.* Retrieved from Stay Safe
    Online: https://staysafeonline.org/cybersecure-business/
Ambrose, C. (2014, October 31). *Gartner Vendor Management.* Retrieved from
    Gartner: https://www.gartner.com/doc/2894817/monitor-key-risk-
    criteria-mitigate
Atkinson, J. R. (2010, May). *Need Speed? Slow Down.* Retrieved March 2016,
    from hbr.org: https://hbr.org/2010/05/need-speed-slow-down
Bateman, J. 2020. "War, Terrorism, and Catastrophe in Cyber Insurance:
    Understanding and Reforming Exclusions" Carnegie Endowment for
    International Peace. https://carnegieendowment.org/files/Bateman_-
    _Cyber_Insurance_-_Final.pdf
Bisson, D. (2015, September 23). *The State of Security.* Retrieved from Tripwire:
    http://www.tripwire.com/state-of-security/risk-based-security-for-
    executives/connecting-security-to-the-business/the-top-10-tips-for-
    building-an-effective-security-dashboard/
California, S. o. (2018). *California Consumer Privacy Act (CCPA).* Retrieved from
    https://oag.ca.gov/privacy/ccpa
Chickowski, E. (2016, March 16). *Dark Reading: Analytics.* Retrieved from
    Information Week, DarkReading website:
    http://www.darkreading.com/analytics/10-ways-to-measure-it-security-
    program-effectiveness/d/d-id/1319494
Cichonski, P., Millar, T., Grance, T., & Scarfone, K. (2012, August 23). *Special
    Publications: NIST Pubs.* Retrieved from National Institute of Standards
    and Technology web site:

http://nvlpubs.nist.gov/nistpubs/SpecialPublications/NIST.SP.800-61r2.pdf

CIS. (2000). *CIS Critical Security Controls*. Retrieved from SANS.org: http://www.sans.org/critical-security-controls/

CIS. (2010, November 11). *CIS Consensus Information Security Metrics*. Retrieved June 11, 2016, from Center for Internet Security: https://benchmarks.cisecurity.org/downloads/metrics/#progress

CIS. (2015, October 15). *CIS Controls for Effective Cyber Defense ver 6.0*. Retrieved June 11, 2016, from Center for Internet Security, CIS Critical Controls: https://www.cisecurity.org/critical-controls/

CIS Benchmarks. (2020, January). Retrieved from https://www.cisecurity.org/cis-benchmarks/

CIS Controls. (2019). Retrieved from Center for Internet Security: https://www.cisecurity.org/controls/

CMMI Institute. (2002). *About CMMI Institute*. Retrieved June 10, 2016, from CMMI Institute: http://cmmiinstitute.com/about-cmmi-institute

Commission, F. C. (2019). *Cyberplanner*. Retrieved from https://www.fcc.gov/cyberplanner

Commission, E. (2016). *Data protection in the EU*. Retrieved from https://ec.europa.eu/info/law/law-topic/data-protection/data-protection-eu_en

Commission, F. T. (2019). *Start with Security: A Guide for Business*. Retrieved from https://www.ftc.gov/tips-advice/business-center/guidance/start-security-guide-business

Council, P. S. (2018, May). *PCI DSS*. Retrieved from https://www.pcisecuritystandards.org/document_library

DBR, V. (2019). *2019 DBIR*. Retrieved from Verizon: https://enterprise.verizon.com/resources/reports/2019-data-breach-investigations-report.pdf

Deloitte Development, LLC. (2015). *Cybersecurity and the role of internal audit: An urgent call to action*. Retrieved March 2016, from Deloitte University Press: http://www2.deloitte.com/content/dam/Deloitte/us/Documents/risk/us-risk-cyber-ia-urgent-call-to-action.pdf

Dr. Vincent Hu. (2018). *Access Control Policy and Implementation Guides*. Retrieved from Computer Security Resource Center: https://csrc.nist.gov/Projects/Access-Control-Policy-and-Implementation-Guides

Economic Espionage Act, 18 U.S.C. Ch. 90 § 1839. (1996). *United States Code Title 18 Chapter 90 Section 1839, Economic Espionage Act of 1996*. (O. o. Revision, Ed.) Washington, DC, United States of America: Government Printing Office.

Bibliography

FDIC. (2008, June 6). *Guidance For Managing Third-Party Risk*. Retrieved June 10, 2016, from Federal Deposit Insurance Corporation: https://www.fdic.gov/news/news/financial/2008/fil08044a.html

Foley & Lardner LLP. . (2015, March 11). *Intelligence: Taking Control of Cyber Security*. Retrieved June 11, 2016, from Foley & Lardner LLP : https://www.foley.com/taking-control-of-cybersecurity-a-practical-guide-for-officers-and-directors-03-11-2015/

Greenwald, J. (2014, September 14). *Home Depot has $105 million in cyber insurance to cover data breach*. Retrieved from Business Insurance: http://www.businessinsurance.com/article/20140914/NEWS07/309149975

Gunter K. Stahl, e. a. (2012). Six Principles of Effective Global Talent Management. *MIT Sloan Management review, 53*(2), p. 10.

IAPP. (2016). *Information Systems Access Policy*. Retrieved from https://iapp.org/media/pdf/resource_center/AWPHD-ISaccess.pdf

Ponemon Institute (2017, September 22). Retrieved from PRNEWSWIRE: https://www.prnewswire.com/news-releases/2017-ponemon-institute-study-finds-smbs-are-a-huge-target-for-hackers-300521423.html

ISACA. (2019). *COBIT 5*. Retrieved from https://cobitonline.isaca.org/about

ISO. (2015, December 31). *Information security management*. Retrieved from International Organization for Standardization (ISO). Retrieved June 11, 2016, from ISO/IEC 27001 - Information security management: http://www.iso.org/iso/home/standards/management-standards/iso27001.htm

ITIL. (1988). *ITIL Open Guide*. Retrieved 2016, from IT Library: http://itlibrary.org/

Johnston, R., Jones, A., Dempsey, K., Chawla, N., Jones, A., Orebaugh, A., . . . Stine, K. (2011, September 30). *NIST: Special Publications*. Retrieved from NIST, U.S. Department of Commerce Website: http://nvlpubs.nist.gov/nistpubs/Legacy/SP/nistspecialpublication800-137.pdf

LSE. (2019). *Information Security Policy*. Retrieved from London School of Economics and Political Science: https://info.lse.ac.uk/staff/services/Policies-and-procedures/Assets/Documents/infSecPol.pdf

CSO Magazine (2016, January 25). *Security*. Retrieved from https://www.csoonline.com/article/3019126/security-policy-samples-templates-and-tools.html

CSO Magazine (2018, May). *Cyber-resilient*. Retrieved from Adaptive Security: https://www.csoonline.com/article/3273346/what-should-a-cyber-resilient-business-look-like.html

MITRE. (2011, September). *Cyber Resiliency Engineering Framework*. Retrieved from https://www.mitre.org/sites/default/files/pdf/11_4436.pdf

Mohamed, A. (2013). *Data classification: why it is important and how to do it.* Retrieved from ComputerWeekly: http://www.computerweekly.com/feature/Data-classification-why-it-is-important-and-how-to-do-it

National Institute of Standards and Technology. (2014, February 12). *Framework for Improving Critical Infrastructure Cybersecurity.* Retrieved June 11, 2016, from National Institute of Standards and Technology: http://www.nist.gov/cyberframework/upload/cybersecurity-framework-021214.pdf

NIST. (2004, February). FIPS PUB 199. *Standards for Security Categorization of Federal Information and Information Systems.* Gaithersburg, MD, United States: National Institute of Standards and Technology.

NIST. (2014, February 12). *Framework for Improving Critical Infrastructure Cybersecurity.* Retrieved from National Institute of Standards and Technology Web Site: http://www.nist.gov/cyberframework/upload/cybersecurity-framework-021214.pdf

NIST. (2015). *Security & Privacy Controls.* Retrieved from Computer Science Resource Center: https://csrc.nist.gov/publications/detail/sp/800-53/rev-4/final

NIST. (2017, June). *An Introduction to Information Security.* Retrieved from Computer Security Resource Center: https://csrc.nist.gov/publications/detail/sp/800-12/rev-1/final

NIST. (2018, December). *RMF.* Retrieved from Computer Security Resource Center: https://csrc.nist.gov/publications/detail/sp/800-37/rev-2/final

NIST. (2019). *Cybersecurity Framework.* Retrieved from Resources: https://www.us-cert.gov/resources/cybersecurity-framework

NIST. (2019, November). *Developing Cyber Resilient Systems.* Retrieved from Computer Security Resource Center: https://csrc.nist.gov/publications/detail/sp/800-160/vol-2/final

NIST 800-30 r1. (2012, September). *Guide for Conducting Risk Assessments.* Retrieved June 2016, from NVLPUBS.NIST.GOV: http://nvlpubs.nist.gov/nistpubs/Legacy/SP/nistspecialpublication800-30r1.pdf

PCI-DSS. (2006). *Payment Card Industry Data Security Standards.* Retrieved June 2016, from PCI Security Standards Council: https://www.pcisecuritystandards.org/

Pink, D. H. (2009). *Drive: The Surprising Truth About What Motivates Us.* New York, NY, USA: Riverhead Hardcover.

Ponemon Institute. (2018). *2018 State of SMB Cybersecurity.* Retrieved from https://start.keeper.io/2018-ponemon-report

Ponemon Institute. (2019, June 15). *IBM Security.* Retrieved from Collaboration: https://www.ibm.com/security/data-breach?cm_sp=CTO-_-en-US-_-ZBZLY7KL

Porath, T. S. (2014, May 30). Why You Hate Work. *New Your Times*, p. 5.

Raptis, S. (2015, March 13). *Cyber Risk: Analyzing Cyber Risk Coverage*. Retrieved from Risk and Insurance: http://www.riskandinsurance.com/analyzing-cyber-risk-coverage/

SANS. (2009). *Gathering Security Metrics*. Retrieved from Information Security Reading Room: https://www.sans.org/reading-room/whitepapers/leadership/gathering-security-metrics-reaping-rewards-33234

SANS. (2019). *Information Security Policy Templates*. Retrieved from SANS Security Policy Research: https://www.sans.org/security-resources/policies

Center for Information Security, (2016, March 01). *CIS CONSENSUS INFORMATION SECURITY METRICS*. Retrieved from Center for Internet Security: https://benchmarks.cisecurity.org/downloads/metrics/

Center for Information Security (2019). *CIS Benchmarks*. Retrieved from https://learn.cisecurity.org/benchmarks

ThreatTrack Security, (2014, December 13). *ThreatTrack Whitepapers*. Retrieved from ThreatTrack Security Inc.: http://www.threattracksecurity.com/resources/white-papers/chief-information-security-officers-misunderstood.aspx

Cybersecurity & Infrastructure Security Agency (2019, November). *Avoiding Social Engineering and Phishing Attacks*. Retrieved from Tips: https://www.us-cert.gov/ncas/tips/ST04-014

Cybersecurity & Infrastructure Security Agency (2019). *Enhanced Cybersecurity Services (ECS)*. Retrieved from Information Sharing: https://www.dhs.gov/cisa/enhanced-cybersecurity-services-ecs

Cybersecurity & Infrastructure Security Agency (2019). *Home and Business Security Resources*. Retrieved from CIS Resources: https://www.us-cert.gov/home-and-business

Cybersecurity & Infrastructure Security Agency (2019). *Resources*. Retrieved from CISA: https://www.us-cert.gov/resources

Cybersecurity & Infrastructure Security Agency (2019). *Resources for Business*. Retrieved from Resources: https://www.us-cert.gov/resources/business

Cybersecurity & Infrastructure Security Agency (2019). *Resources for Small and Midsize Businesses (SMB)*. Retrieved from cybersecurity resources and best practices for businesses, government agencies, and other organizations.

Cybersecurity & Infrastructure Security Agency (2019). *Tips*. Retrieved from National Cyber Awareness System: https://www.us-cert.gov/ncas/tips

Seiner, R. S. (2014). *Non-Invasive Data Governance, The Path of Least Resistance and Great Success*. Basking Ridge, NJ: Technics Publications.

Cybersecurity & Infrastructure Security Agency (n.d.). *Health Information Privacy*. Retrieved from 2019: https://www.hhs.gov/hipaa/index.html

Standardization, I. O. (2013). *ISO/IEC 27001 INFORMATION SECURITY MANAGEMENT*. Retrieved from ISO Standards: https://www.iso.org/isoiec-27001-information-security.html

The Santa Fe Strategy Center LTD. (2016). *Standardized Information Gathering Questionnaire*. Retrieved June 13, 2016, from Shared Assessments Member: https://sharedassessments.org/

Tucker Bailey, J. B. (2013, December). *Business Functions: McKinsey&Company*. Retrieved from McKinsey&Company Website: http://www.mckinsey.com/business-functions/business-technology/our-insights/how-good-is-your-cyberincident-response-plan

UCF. (2004). *Unified Compliance Framework*. Retrieved 2016, from Unifiedcompliance.com: https://www.unifiedcompliance.com/

University, C. M. (2015). *Computer Security Incident Response Plan*. Retrieved from Governance: https://www.cmu.edu/iso/governance/procedures/docs/incidentresponseplan1.0.pdf

Wikipedia 2. (2016, March 19). *ITIL security management*. Retrieved June 12, 2016, from wikipedia.org: https://en.wikipedia.org/wiki/ITIL_security_management

Wikipedia. (2016, March 31). *Capability Maturity Model Integration*. Retrieved June 10, 2016, from wikipedia.org: https://en.wikipedia.org/wiki/Capability_Maturity_Model_Integration

Wikipedia. (2016, May 31). *ITIL*. Retrieved June 12, 2016, from wikipedia.org: https://en.wikipedia.org/wiki/ITIL

Wikipedia. (2019, September 30). *Data Privacy Day*. Retrieved from https://en.wikipedia.org/wiki/Data_Privacy_Day

Resources on Zero Trust

- IBM - https://www.ibm.com/topics/zero-trust
- Microsoft - https://www.microsoft.com/en-us/security/business/zero-trust
- NIST - https://nvlpubs.nist.gov/nistpubs/SpecialPublications/NIST.SP.800-207.pdf

Articles on Software Liability

- https://incompliancemag.com/article/technology-developments-and-the-risk-of-product-liability/
- https://scholarship.law.duke.edu/cgi/viewcontent.cgi?article=1322&context=dltr

- https://cs.stanford.edu/people/eroberts/cs181/projects/liability-law/Liability&Neg.html
- https://www.twobirds.com/en/news/articles/2005/liability-for-software-errors

Data Categories and Examples

As you work with your stakeholders, they will need to help you identify key attributes of the data which will help you categorize it. Examples of data categories include:

- Public – data that is publicly releasable
- Internal – internal business information
- Confidential/Private – legal, intellectual property, R&D
- Restricted/Controlled – compliance related (PII, PHI, NPI)
- Secret – protects or controls access to data (keys, passwords)

Definitions for these general classes of information are as follows:

- **Public** – Information that can be publicly disclosed. Public information is information that has been approved for public release, created with the intention of being consumed by the general public, or can be found through sources generally available to the public. The key characteristic of information that can be classified as Public is that there is no risk (brand, financial, operational, competitive) in the public disclosure of the information.

- **Internal** – Information not approved for general circulation outside the organization, but suitable for general circulation within the organization. The key characteristics of information that can be classified as Internal are that public disclosure would inconvenience the organization or management but would be unlikely to result in financial loss or serious damage to the brand and that the information can generally be shared within the company without restriction.

- **Confidential/Private** – Information not approved for general circulation outside the organization and controlled within the organization on a need-to-know basis. Confidential information is information that is proprietary to the company and not suitable for general dissemination within the company or information that is derived from a customer relationship. The key characteristics of information that should be classified as Confidential are that public disclosures would be likely to result in modest negative financial outcomes or impact to the brand (including customer trust) and that the information is not suitable for general dissemination within the company.

- **Intellectual Property** – Also called: "Intellectual Capital," "Proprietary Information," and "Trade Secrets." This includes data elements such as design plans for the organization's next generation products, customer and prospect lists, detailed sales forecasts, and salary structures. Also, production methodologies, secret formulas, processes, and methods used in production, business and marketing plans, contracts, and details of your computer systems. In some cases, the specialized knowledge and skills that an employee has learned on the job are considered to be an organization's proprietary information. The term "trade secret" also includes all forms and types of financial, business, scientific, technical, economic, or engineering information. Included are patterns, plans, compilations, program devices, formulas, designs, prototypes, methods, techniques, processes, procedures, programs, or codes, whether tangible or intangible, and whether or how stored, compiled, or memorialized physically, electronically, graphically, photographically, or in writing.

- The Economic Espionage Act of 1996 (EEA), which was modeled on the Uniform Trade Secrets Act (UTSA) (Economic Espionage Act, 18 U.S.C. Ch. 90 § 1839, 1996) defines what an organization can or should classify as trade secrets. It also establishes the behavioral criteria to extend the cloak of legislative protection over what the organization designates as proprietary information or trade secrets. In essence, organizations must take reasonable measures to keep the information secret, and its existence as a secret or as something not generally known must give the organization an economic or competitive benefit.

- **Operational Data** – Traditionally, this includes production output figures, resource utilization, environmental data for physical systems, and process load, storage capacity, and memory utilization for virtual machines. Goals for handling most operational data focus on integrity and availability. A word of caution is in order. Given the advent of ubiquitous data analytics and the rapid adoption of IoT (and the vast array of sensors that makes IoT work), the competitive intelligence gained by intercepting and analyzing seemingly low-sensitivity operational data has increased exponentially. Some industries have already matured to a state where the confidentiality of all operational data is as important as the integrity and availability of that data.

- **Restricted/Controlled** – Information whose handling is dictated, influenced, or suggested through law, regulation, or contract, or that is considered critical to the organization's strategy or ongoing operation. The key characteristics of information that must be classified as Restricted/Controlled are that unauthorized disclosure of this information is likely to result in serious negative financial outcomes, loss of customer trust, damage to the brand, regulatory penalties, civil or criminal complaint, or a strategic disadvantage for the company.

- **Non-Public Information (NPI)** – This is addressed specifically in the Gramm-Leach-Bliley Act (GLBA) and defined as name, address, social security number (SSN) or other information provided on an application (typically with a financial services firm). This information is governed by the Act's Privacy Rule, which limits activity related to NPI without notification. Concerning GLBA, if the information is reasonably available in the public domain, it is no longer classified as NPI. There is also a concept of the combination of unique data elements (e.g., name + address) creating NPI in specific contexts.

- **Material Non-Public Information (MNPI)** - Material Non-public Information is information that would affect the market value or trading of a security and that has not been disseminated to the general public. Information is considered to be "material" if its dissemination to the public would likely affect the market value or trading price of an issuer's securities, or if it is information which, if disclosed, would likely influence a reasonable investor's decision to purchase or sell an issuer's securities.

- **Personally Identifiable Information (PII)** – The National Institute of Standards and Technology (NIST) Special Publication 800-122, "Guide to Protecting the Confidentiality of Personally Identifiable Information (PII)," leverages the 2008 Government Accounting Office's (GAO's) definition of PII. It stated as follows: "any information about an individual maintained by an agency, including (1) any information that can be used to distinguish or trace an individual's identity, such as name, social security number, date and place of birth, mother's maiden name, or biometric records; and (2) any other information that is linked or linkable to an individual, such as medical, educational, financial, and employment information."[24] The definitions of both PII and NPI are used widely by states for their breach notification laws.

- **Protected Health Information (PHI)** – Title 45 C.F.R. § 160.103 defines PHI as individually identifiable health information. PHI is effectively any information in the health record of an individual that makes that individual uniquely identifiable. PHI could include billing information (e.g., name and address) as well as procedural information (e.g., tests, scans, or results from other medical procedures that create information uniquely attributable to the individual).

- **Electronic Protected Health Information (ePHI)** – ePHI is effectively the electronic equivalent of PHI. The Health Information Technology for Economic and Clinical Health Act (HITECH) cemented ePHI's prominence in healthcare. This act provided government incentives to convert medical records into electronic health records (EHRs). HIPAA-HITECH governs how covered entities (typically hospitals and insurance companies) share PHI and ePHI with business associates (third parties) that deliver services required to provide health care. Both PHI and ePHI are subject to the HIPAA Security and Privacy Rules.

- **Credit Card Data** – The Payment Card Industry (PCI) defines different data elements related to the ubiquitous credit card. Cardholder data is the PII related to the end-user,

---

[24] NIST Special Publication 800-122 found at: http://csrc.nist.gov/publications/nistpubs/800-122/sp800-122.pdf.

including data elements such as the name, address, phone number, and the primary account number (PAN). Additionally, PCI provides guidance and definitions related to card validation codes. The Payment Card Industry Data Security Standard (PCI-DSS) provides required security measures associated with protecting this information.

- **Secret** – Information that is used to protect access to multiple records of information classified as Confidential/Private, and Restricted/Controlled or single or multiple records of Secret data. The key characteristics of information that must be classified as Secret are that unauthorized disclosure of this information is likely to result in severe negative financial outcomes, loss of customer trust, damage to the brand, regulatory penalties, civil or criminal complaint, or a strategic disadvantage for the company.

    Encryption keys, passwords, certificates, and other cryptographic data elements used in the process of securing access and data.

Sometimes the same information fits into more than one category. Salary information about an individual, for instance, may be considered private information and protecting it may be a matter of privacy. Salary ranges across a division may be proprietary information the company wishes to keep confidential to protect trade advantages they gain from labor arbitrage.

What is significant about all of this is to establish a foundation for identifying the data over which an organization has control. The organization should then assume responsibility for protecting this data from inappropriate use or disclosure. Inappropriate meaning without the authorization of a data custodian charged with protecting that data and, when applicable, the explicit permission of the data subject.

Determining the value of this information, and the associated and commensurate security and governance practices, is a process that requires the CISO to be fully engaged with colleagues across the organization ... certainly beyond traditional IT counterparts. Valued participants in this assessment include other C-level executives, corporate counsel, line-of-business executives, and the board as well as business partners, vendors and, potentially, regulatory authorities who may have legally mandated expectations regarding how the organization manages certain types of information.

Acknowledgements

Bill Bonney: I would like to thank my wife, Nadine, for her loving support. She has always been my biggest fan and a source of constant strength. Thank you to my partner, Christine, for the special bond that I have come to cherish and depend on for joy and inspiration.

Gary Hayslip: I would like to tell my wife of 25 years, Sandi, thank you for your patience and calming influence. Your love and support have allowed me to stay focused on this project. You are my best friend and I thank you for putting up with my late-night rewrites and rambling debates.

Matt Stamper: I want to acknowledge and thank my family…especially my wife Lisa and our daughters Lauren and Danielle. Their patience with me cannot be overstated. I am also indebted to my parents for giving me a love of learning.

Collectively, we are grateful for the support and camaraderie from our colleagues in the San Diego Information Security community, especially ISACA, InfraGard, and the members of the San Diego CISO Round Table.

Finally, the authors wish to thank the members of the cybersecurity community, whose readership, feedback, and encouragement have helped make the *CISO Desk Reference Guide Executive Primer* a reality. We have been humbled and honored to receive feedback from all corners of the world and thrilled that our books have sold in sixteen countries and counting.

Thank you to Allan Alford, Kirsten Davies, Dr. John Sahlin, and Bob Zukis for your time to review *The CISO Desk Reference Guide Executive Primer* and provide thoughtful and invaluable feedback.

About the Authors

Bill Bonney is a security evangelist, author, and consultant. As co-author of the Cybersecurity Canon Hall of Fame books the *CISO Desk Reference Guide: A Practical Guide for CISOs – Volumes 1 and 2*, Bill is dedicated to providing the practical advice needed  to combat the ongoing scourge of cybercrime. Prior to co-founding CISO DRG Publishing, Bill was Vice President of Product Marketing and Chief Strategist at UBIQ, a maker of high-speed encryption software, Vice President of Product Marketing and Principal Consulting Analyst at TechVision Research, and Director of Information Security and Compliance at Intuit, maker of personal and small business financial products.

Bill holds multiple patents in data protection, access, and classification, and was a founding member of the board of directors for the San Diego CISO Round Table, a professional group focused on building relationships and fostering collaboration in information security management. Bill is a highly regarded speaker and panelist addressing technology and security concerns. In addition to co-authoring the two volumes of the *CISO Desk Reference Guide*, Bill has also written *Bring Your Own Cyber, A Small Business Owner's Guide to Basic Network Security* to help extremely small companies improve their security. He holds a Bachelor of Science degree in Computer Science and Applied Mathematics from Albany University.

LinkedIn Profile: https://www.linkedin.com/in/billbonney

Matt Stamper, CISA, CISM, CRISC, CDPSE, CIPP-US. As a senior security leader with both public and early-stage company experience, Matt brings a broad, multi-disciplinary knowledge of privacy and cybersecurity best practices to his clients. His diverse domain expertise spans IT service management (ITSM), cybersecurity, cloud services, control design and assessment (Sarbanes-Oxley, HIPAA-HITECH), privacy (GDPR, CCPA, CPRA), governance, enterprise risk, and IT risk management (ERM/ITRM). Matt is a co-author of the *CISO Desk Reference Guide, Volumes 1 and 2*, which he wrote with Hayslip and Bonney.

Matt's diverse experience also includes sales management and individual revenue contribution, new product and service development, and international experience in both Latin America and China. Matt excels at conveying complex privacy, cybersecurity, and IT concepts to boards of directors, executive management, and professional service providers. His executive-level experience with managed services, cybersecurity, data centers, networks services, and ITSM provides a unique perspective on the fast-changing world of enterprise IT, IoT, and cloud services. Matt has served as a Security Analyst and Research Director at Gartner and in multiple CISOs roles. Matt is an IT Sector Chief for the FBI InfraGard program and a member of the Board of the San Diego ISACA chapter.

Matt received a Bachelor of Arts from the University of California at San Diego, graduating Cum Laude and with Honors and Distinction in Political Science. He earned a Master of Arts in Pacific International Affairs from the University of California at San Diego and a Master of Science degree in Telecommunications sponsored by AT&T. He is fluent in Spanish and has worked in executive roles in Latin America.

LinkedIn Profile: https://www.linkedin.com/in/stamper

About the Authors

With over 20 years of IT, Cybersecurity, and Risk Management experience, Gary Hayslip has established a reputation as a highly skilled communicator, author, and keynote speaker. Currently, as Chief Information Security Officer for Softbank Investment Advisers (SBIA), he advises executive leadership on protecting critical information resources and overseeing enterprise cybersecurity strategy. Hayslip co-authored the *CISO Desk Reference Guide: A Practical Guide for CISOs – Volumes 1 and 2*, which enable CISOs to expand their business and leadership expertise. Hayslip recently published the *Essential Guide to Cybersecurity for SMBs*, a practical guidebook for the SMB security professional and coauthored *Develop Your Cybersecurity Career Path: How to Break into Cybersecurity at Any Level*. Hayslip's previous executive experience includes multiple CISO, CIO, Deputy Director of IT and Chief Privacy Officer roles for the U.S. Navy (Active Duty), the U.S. Navy (Federal Government employee), the City of San Diego California, and Webroot Software.

LinkedIn Profile: https://www.linkedin.com/in/ghayslip/

Made in the USA
Las Vegas, NV
10 March 2024